Stop Me Because I Can't Stop Myself

Stop Me Because I Can't Stop Myself

Taking Control of Impulsive Behavior

Jon E. Grant, J.D., M.D.

and

S. W. Kim, M.D.

McGraw-Hill

New York   Chicago   San Francisco   Lisbon   London   Madrid   Mexico City
Milan   New Delhi   San Juan   Seoul   Singapore   Sydney   Toronto

The *McGraw-Hill* Companies

Library of Congress Cataloging-in-Publication Data

Grant, Jon E.
  Stop me because I can't stop myself : taking control of impulsive
behavior / by Jon E. Grant and Suck Won Kim.
    p. ; cm.
Includes bibliographical references and index.
  ISBN 0-07-139826-0 (hardcover : alk. paper)
1. Impulse control disorders.
  [DNLM: 1. Impulse Control Disorders—psychology. . Impulse Control
Disorders—therapy. WM 190 G7625s 2003] I. Kim, Suck Won. II. Title.
  RC569.5.I46 G73 2003
  616.85'84—dc21   2002011489

1 2 3 4 5   DOH/DOH   15 14 13

ISBN 0-07-139826-0

McGraw-Hill books are available at special quantity discounts to use as premiums and sales promotions, or for use in corporate training programs. For more information, please write to the Director of Special Sales, Professional Publishing, McGraw-Hill, Two Penn Plaza, New York, NY 10121-2298. Or contact your local bookstore.

All patient names in this book are fictional. To protect confidentiality, the stories are composites of several people's stories. Furthermore, details have been changed to protect patients.

This book is printed on recycled, acid-free paper containing a minimum of 50% recycled, de-inked fiber.

This book is dedicated to our patients
without whom we would never have
learned about the complexity and
severity of these disorders

Contents

Acknowledgments

Although only two of us wrote this book, the thoughts, support, and previous scholarly work of so many people contributed to the creation of this work.

We thank the many colleagues who have contributed, in various ways, to our current knowledge of these disabling disorders: Drs. Carlos Blanco of Columbia University, Donald Black of the University of Iowa, Marc Potenza of Yale University, Renee Cunningham-Williams of Washington University, Eric Hollander of Mount Sinai School of Medicine, Susan McElroy of the University of Cincinnati, Peter Kalivas of Washington State University, the late Gordon Mogenson of the University of Western Ontario, Marcus Goldman of Harvard University, Nancy Raymond of the University of Minnesota, and Eli Coleman of the University of Minnesota.

We also thank our many friends and mentors who have fostered the love of research and provided invaluable support over many years: Dr. Katharine A. Phillips of Butler Hospital and Brown University School of Medicine, Drs. Paula J. Clayton and S. Charles Schulz of the University of Minnesota, Drs. Boyd Hartman and Patricia Faris of the University of Minnesota, Dr. Pedro Ramirez of the University of Alabama, Rebecca L. Grosz, our research coordinator, and a very special thanks to Patricia Perkins Doyle, J.D., of the Obsessive Compulsive Foundation, a fellow attorney in a world of physicians.

The following organizations have provided support without which this book would not have been possible: Obsessive Compulsive Foundation, National Center for Responsible Gaming, and the University of Minnesota Medical School.

We thank those people who read portions of the manuscript and provided thoughtful comments: Drs. S. Charles Schulz, Jerome Kroll, Thomas A. Mackenzie, Gary Christenson, David Opsahl, Paul Erickson, Yvonne Sturm, and Clark Peters, Esq., and Leslie Barnhart, Esq.

And finally, we express appreciation to our editors at McGraw-Hill, Susan Clarey and Nancy Hancock, and their entire staff, who provided boundless energy and enthusiasm for our project. Their attention to detail truly has made it a work worthy of the people whose struggles we attempt to portray.

Introduction

Most of us have urges to engage in behaviors that we know may not be good for us. We might gamble while on vacation in Las Vegas, we might splurge on gifts for our family during the holidays even when we don't have enough money, or we might take the towels home from the hotel to remember a vacation. The behaviors seen in impulse control disorders are like these, but extreme versions. People with impulse control disorders not only engage in extreme behaviors, but also feel that their urges to do so are uncontrollable. Because of the intense urges associated with these behaviors, people with impulse control disorders often become preoccupied with the behaviors. They would like to stop these behaviors, but they are unable to do so. One man told us, "I don't feel like I have control over my actions any longer. Please stop me, because I can't stop myself."

People who engage in impulsive behavior usually suffer intense emotional distress. Kimberly, who suffered from compulsive sexual behavior, described herself as an "evil person." Mark, a compulsive shopper, characterized himself as "weak and pathetic." Additionally, both the urges and the behaviors associated with impulse control disorders may significantly interfere with people's lives. Leslie, who had a problem with pathological gambling, was sometimes late for work after being at the casino all night. She often missed social activities with friends because she preferred to go to the casino alone.

Although they cause severe emotional distress, impulse control disorders often remain secret because many people seem to function fairly well despite their distress—they work, raise families, and spend time with friends. Often no one knows how tormented and unhappy these people are. Susan was tormented daily by her urges to steal. Yet, she continued to work well at a high-level job and had a good marriage. Although Brandon was gambling almost daily and was preoccupied with his feelings of guilt, he continued to do his job well and raise his two children.

When impulse control disorders are severe, however, the normal ability to function is impaired. Friendships, relationships, and work suffer. Margaret was so consumed by her shopping that she stopped working, wouldn't see her friends, and ultimately lost her marriage. Because of the debt she incurred while shopping, Margaret was broke; she lost her savings and her house, had to live with her children, and thought about suicide daily.

Impulse control disorders are often difficult for people, even those who suffer from them, to understand. Why don't these people just stop doing these things if the behavior bothers them so much? One woman described her struggle with her own behavior: "I keep asking myself why I can't stop stealing. I have plenty of money to buy the stuff, and I get so depressed after I steal something. I usually spend the next couple of days locked in my room crying. I hate myself for not being able to control this behavior."

Of the many mental disorders we have treated, impulse control disorders (pathological gambling, compulsive sexual behavior, kleptomania, and compulsive shopping) are among the most shame-provoking and devastating problems we have encountered. Distressed by their lack of control over their behavior, and yet too ashamed to tell others, these people suffer in silence.

Impulse control disorders can have a significant impact not only on the person with the illness, but also on his or her family, friends, and coworkers. Watching a loved one suffer and feeling incapable of helping that person can take an emotional toll on anyone. Even when family and friends know what the problem is, they are often at a loss to know what they can do to help. Other times, because of the shame and secrecy associated with these disorders, family and friends don't even know what the problem is. They may be aware that a loved one is experiencing psychological distress or avoiding certain activities, but be unaware that an impulse control disorder is the cause. People with impulse control disorders are often too embarrassed to discuss their difficulties, even with their closest friends.

Many people with impulse control disorders will not share their secret out of fear that others will think they are crazy or will condemn their behavior. One woman had never told her husband that she had been gambling two nights a week for the past two to three years. "He wouldn't understand. He's so responsible. If he knew I had lost our savings, he would be upset. I love him, but I'm not able to share this—I'm too embarrassed." Another man had been stealing weekly for thirty years and his wife had never known. "How can I admit to doing something like this? I hate myself for not having any control. I don't want my wife to hate me."

Although people may delay actually performing the various behaviors, the urges to perform them do not seem to diminish over time. In fact, the urges may become uncontrollable. And when they do, the resulting behaviors may lead to overwhelming problems for both the individual and his or her family and friends. Todd stole from his family to find money for the casino. Jennifer lied to her husband, saying she was going to work when in fact she was shopping almost every day. Impulse control disorders are illnesses, but the consequences of the behaviors may be difficult for family or friends to accept.

The fact that the behaviors are often kept secret from family and friends only compounds the shame and embarrassment that those who suffer from these illnesses feel. Many people with impulse control disorders feel that they are responsible for the behavior that seems to be destroying them and their families. They may also worry that professionals will blame them for their behavior, and so they rarely tell their physicians about their difficulties.

Although these diseases are virtually unknown to the American public, impulse control disorders have been described for centuries. Historical evidence suggests that some form of pathological gambling was a problem in time periods and cultures as diverse as ancient Rome, nineteenth-century Russia, and colonial America. The disorder now known as kleptomania first appeared in the medical literature in the eighteenth century in the case of a wealthy woman who was facing criminal charges for theft. In 1838 the disorder was given the name *kleptomania*, and it received a large amount of attention in response to what appeared to be an epidemic of young women stealing clothing from stores in Paris, France. The nineteenth century also saw the beginning of medical literature addressing compulsive sexual behavior; *satyrism* and *nymphomania* were early terms for this illness. And finally, compulsive shopping dates back at least to the nineteenth century in America. There has been speculation that Mary Todd Lincoln may have suffered from compulsive shopping after the death of her husband. At that time, *oniomania* was the term used to describe this disorder, and psychiatrists as famous as Emil Kraeplin were attempting to find treatments for it. What these examples demonstrate is that impulse control disorders are not new. For centuries, people all over the world have been suffering from these illnesses.

Impulse control disorders are not uncommon. The medical community fails to recognize and diagnose these disorders, in part, because of the patient's embarrassment, shame, and inability to discuss the problem. How common are these disorders? Preliminary estimates suggest that these disorders, taken together, may affect as many as 3 to 15 percent of the U.S. population (approximately 8 to 35 million people). People of all socioeconomic classes suffer from impulse control disorders. These illnesses also occur in people around the world.

Impulse control disorders cause significant suffering and yet are virtually unknown by physicians, the public, and even those who suffer from these illnesses. We wrote this book to provide understanding and help for those who suffer from and for those who treat impulse control disorders. We have treated hundreds of people who suffer from these disorders. Although there is still much that we do not know about these life-limiting disorders, our patients' repeated requests for information convinced us to write this book.

This book focuses on certain specific impulse control disorders: pathological gambling, compulsive shopping, kleptomania (compulsive shoplifting), and compulsive sexual behavior. Are there other disorders, not included in this book, that could be called impulse control problems? Yes, there are. The decision to exclude various illnesses that involve impulsivity (for example, substance use disorders, trichotillomania, skin picking, nail biting, compulsive computer use, and pyromania/fire setting) was based on two factors. First, the disorders we will discuss are defined by people's urges for certain rewards—items purchased, stolen, or won and sexual experiences. There is a desired object that is rewarding to the people who suffer from these illnesses. Unlike trichotillomania and skin picking, which involve a desire for anxiety reduction, the illnesses we present have clear rewarding aspects to the behaviors.

The second reason for the particular focus of this book is that the disorders we address, while arguably as disabling as the excluded illnesses, have received little attention in either the popular press or the scientific literature. Substance use disorders (alcoholism and drug use) and trichotillomania, on the other hand, have been well studied and extensively covered by other writers. Although skin picking, nail biting, compulsive computer use, and pyromania deserve the attention of both clinicians and researchers, we see too few cases of these illnesses to make meaningful comments. Although we specialize in treating the disorders presented here, we will inevitably use knowledge of these excluded illnesses to shed light on the impulse control disorders we discuss. Although each disorder would require an entire book to grapple fully with its complexities, we believe our modest contribution will enable others to recognize, seek help for, and receive proper treatment for these disorders.

The disorders described in this book are historically grouped under the category of "impulse control disorders." However, how does impulsive behavior differ from obsessive or compulsive behavior? Is something impulsive if a person thinks about doing it all day before he or she actually does it? These are difficult questions, in part, because there are no easy definitions for any of these terms. Many behaviors may start out as impulsive and become compulsive over time. Also, there may be overlap among these terms—urge-based behaviors that appear to be impulsive may preoccupy someone all day and therefore also appear obsessional.

We describe *impulsive* disorders as behaviors driven by urges. The behaviors themselves are usually ego-syntonic; that is, people generally see the behavior as consistent with their will. That does not mean that people want to engage in the behaviors or that the behaviors do not cause problems for these people. In most cases, however, there is a strong drive to perform the behavior that is usually followed, perhaps immediately, by remorse, guilt, or shame.

Compulsive behaviors are usually associated with obsessive-compulsive disorder (OCD). OCD involves a preoccupation with thoughts that are usually ego-dystonic; that is, people are bothered by these thoughts or obsessions. Compulsive behaviors are performed to relieve oneself of these obsessional thoughts. For example, a person may wash repeatedly to relieve himself of thoughts and fears of contamination. Although we will talk about compulsive shopping and compulsive sexual behavior, we believe that these illnesses are in fact impulse control disorders, as they involve urges to shop or engage in sexual activity.

Because of the difficulty with the terminology, we will use the term *impulse control disorders* interchangeably with the recently coined phrase *behavioral addiction*. In fact, behavioral addiction may more adequately describe the way the brain processes the urge to engage in rewarding behavior. We will describe this in more detail in a later chapter.

We will describe what is known about impulse control disorders and what patients experience. Because impulse control disorders are often more extreme versions of normal behavior, we will consider where typical behavior stops and impulse control disorders begin. We will also tackle several other difficult questions: What causes these illnesses, why are some people more impulsive than others, how do I know if I or someone I care about has an impulse control disorder, and what treatments are available?

Many of our patients believed that no one else in the world suffered from similar problems. Many of them did not know that the problems they had been struggling with for years had names and available treatments. Education on impulse control disorders may be effective in removing the stigma, shame, and loneliness that people with these illnesses feel. With greater education, particularly concerning available treatments, people with impulse control disorders may be more willing to seek treatment for their illnesses. We can all benefit from understanding impulse control disorders and learning to identify them when they appear in our lives or in the lives of friends or family members. Nearly everyone has a friend, relative, or acquaintance whose life is touched by an impulse control disorder. The closer one is to these disorders, the more one knows about how distressing and destructive they can be.

These illnesses afflict millions in our society and around the world. We hope that people who suffer from these disorders and their family members will use this book to seek proper treatment. There are professionals who are willing to help. There is no reason for secrecy, shame, or embarrassment. We stress to every patient we care for that there is hope for those who suffer from impulse control disorders.

1

Stories of Behavioral Addictions

Robert: The Story of a Pathological Gambler

"I've lost everything," Robert began as he took a seat in my office. "It's out of control. I can't think of anything but gambling. Even though I keep losing, I want to return to the casino and try to win back my money." Robert was noticeably upset—unable to look me in the eye, almost on the point of tears. He had called a few weeks earlier wanting to come in, but had kept finding excuses to put off the appointment. During the initial phone conversation, he refused to give me his name because of the shame and embarrassment he felt. After three phone calls, he finally made an appointment for an evening when he felt no one would see him entering a psychiatrist's office.

At first, Robert was reluctant to disclose details about his gambling. "I should be able to stop on my own. I'm not even sure why I'm here. You're a psychiatrist. I don't think I'm crazy. I just need to exercise more willpower. Other people seem to be able to go to the casino, stay a little while, and leave. I don't know why I can't seem to pull myself away once I get there. It's embarrassing."

Robert went on to discuss how he had started gambling during college. He would often bet on sporting events with friends. His gambling was sporadic and apparently did not cause any problems in his life. Over the next three or four years, he started going to the local casino every couple of months with friends and playing blackjack. He would occasionally win, but even if he lost, he was able to return home without being preoccupied by the experience.

Now twenty-seven years old, Robert remembers fairly distinctly when gambling started becoming a problem for him. "I guess it was some time last year when I didn't want to go to the casino with my friends. I wanted to go alone. I felt that if there were fewer distractions, I could concentrate on the cards and would have a better chance of winning. I realized at that time that gambling was no longer a game to me—it was controlling me." He fidgeted in his chair and looked uncomfortable. "It sounds like I'm an addict or something. I have never had a problem with drugs or alcohol, and here I am sounding like I'm hooked on something. The urges I have to gamble are so intense. Is this how drug addicts feel?"

Robert continued to describe how over the past year the amount of time he spent gambling had increased. He was currently going to the casino two or three nights per week. Although he intended to gamble for only a few hours and spend no more than $100 each visit, Robert usually spent most of the evening at the casino and used his credit card once the $100 in cash ran out. Robert often acquired debt of $500 to $1000 per night. The late evenings at the casino made it difficult for him to concentrate at work the next day. "I work in an accounting office. I need to be able to concentrate. After sitting up all night at the casino, I'm in no shape to work. My work has suffered, and my boss is upset." Robert's concentration at work also suffered because of the almost constant thoughts of gambling that preoccupied him. When asked to quantify the amount of time he spent thinking about gambling, Robert replied, "I probably think about my losses or about strategies to win a total of three or four hours each day. It doesn't leave a lot of room for thinking about my work."

I asked Robert why he felt he couldn't stop gambling. "I don't know if you can understand. The cravings I have to gamble are so strong. They take priority over everything else in my life. I can be driving home from work, planning on being with my wife and child for dinner. On the way home, I see a billboard for the casino, and my urges to gamble are triggered. The urges are intense, and I can't resist them. Suddenly, I'm on my way to the casino, calling my wife on the cell phone and telling her I have to stay late at work." Although Robert explained that his urges to gamble were usually triggered by billboards, he had also noticed changes in his urges during the course of his illness. He said that recently he also had urges to gamble immediately upon waking up in the morning. He used to be able to prevent the urges to gamble by taking other routes home after work so that he could avoid the billboards. Now that he was often feeling his urges spontaneously, without a known trigger, Robert felt more "out of control."

"I feel guilty about what I'm doing, but I can't stop. When I get these urges, nothing seems to relieve them except gambling. If I don't get to go to the casino when I have these urges—maybe my wife asks me to do something or a family emergency comes up—I feel incredibly anxious, and I get very irritable. The way I treat my wife and family is sometimes horrible—I leave them alone for hours, I lie to them, I cancel family plans, and it's all due to gambling."

Robert's marriage and his work had both suffered because of his gambling. Although he had been married for only three years, his wife was already talking about divorce. "I think she believes I'm having an affair. She knows nothing about the gambling. I'm ashamed that I'm so weak—I can't tell her. She also doesn't know anything about our debts. I make good money, but the credit card bills are getting bigger. I'm scared I may have to file for bankruptcy." Robert began to cry. "I just keep thinking that if I could win big one time, I would be able to get out of debt and then quit gambling."

While doing his work in the accounting office, Robert spent so much time thinking of ways to win at gambling—which tables to play, how to lay the bets, which "lucky" shirt to wear—that he couldn't complete the projects assigned to him in a timely manner. "I know I have deadlines, and I want to do the work, but I start thinking about gambling and hours just fly by. I can't concentrate on work." Robert also found it difficult to stay at work, even when he had meetings. Instead, when he felt urges to gamble, Robert would leave work early. "I know I'm ruining my career and I just can't stop my behavior."

Before coming to our clinic, Robert had never seen a psychiatrist. He had no history of drug or alcohol abuse or other psychiatric illnesses. When he first came to see me, Robert believed his problem was a lack of willpower, not a psychiatric illness. He didn't really want to see a psychiatrist, but his wife insisted upon it. Although Robert had told no one about his gambling problem, his wife thought he might be suffering from depression. "She told me that I looked sad all the time and that I appeared to be losing weight. When I told her that I just had a checkup with my primary doctor, she suggested I see a psychiatrist.

"The amount of energy, time, and money I have spent gambling has me shaking my head in disgust. I look back and wonder how I have lived this way for the last year or two. It has been unbearable. I have hidden my disease from everyone. I feel like an alcoholic hiding his liquor. I have lived in fear both of the financial repercussions of my gambling and of being discovered. I have hated myself because of this illness. This disease controls you, not the reverse."

Robert's story is typical of what we hear from the pathological gamblers we see in our clinic. Although the symptoms of Robert's gambling problem were severe, his description of his struggle with the illness is what many people with pathological gambling experience. Pathological gambling is an underrecognized and understudied psychiatric disorder in which people are preoccupied with gambling (planning how to win or thinking of past experiences). These people often have no history of other psychiatric problems. They function well in all other respects—holding jobs, having families—until the gambling problem overwhelms their lives.

People with pathological gambling often believe that the problem is one of willpower. If they were to resist the urges to gamble more strongly, they would be able to stop. But they can't stop. Unlike Robert, many people with pathological gambling do not seek psychiatric help. Instead, they tend to blame themselves for the problem. They feel extreme shame and guilt, and they suffer in silence.

In addition to the urges that they feel, pathological gamblers also think about gambling excessively. They worry about their financial problems, and they obsess about winning back their money. This combination of urges and worries causes these people extreme distress. It also interferes substantially with their lives.

Pathological gambling is a complex disorder. How can a person start gambling for fun and then, over time, become unable to stop? Why does this happen to only some people who gamble and not others? How can a person lose thousands of dollars, face bankruptcy, ruin a marriage, jeopardize employment, and yet continue to believe that next time he'll win? Although it is common, pathological gambling is still a poorly understood disorder. Only recently have psychiatrists explored this problem, and the general public is just beginning to hear about pathological gambling. Until recently, the physician did not have much to offer. With recent research on medications and cognitive-behavior therapy, however, there is now hope for people who suffer from pathological gambling.

Gloria: The Story of a Compulsive Shopper

Gloria, a forty-four-year-old married woman, came to see me in the clinic, complaining of feeling depressed. She explained that she had been feeling down for the past several months. She had recently lost her job as a dental assistant and was going through a divorce. When I asked Gloria if there was anything else bothering her, she was silent for several minutes. "It's so embarrassing to talk about. It sounds ridiculous. I think my compulsion to shop is the cause of my depression.

"I don't know when everything got out of control. I've always shopped, but it's only been a problem during the past year—now I'm out of control." Gloria struggled to explain. "I used to go to stores, take my shopping list, get the items, and go home. Every now and then I would buy a few extra 'fun' things, but nothing too extravagant. My husband and I are doing well financially, but both of us are careful about our spending. About a year ago, my husband started to comment that the 'fun' things I was purchasing had increased in number, frequency, and expense. Shortly after that, I noticed that I was going to stores more often than I really needed. I would tell myself that I deserved certain things or that we had plenty of money and so I could afford them. I didn't need or even want the items I was buying—I seemed to be shopping just to shop. I had urges just to purchase something. At first I bought small items— scarves, books, shoes. As time went on, I needed to buy more expensive items to stop the urges—even items I didn't want. I started buying jewelry that I didn't wear and expensive home furnishings (drapes, appliances) that I didn't use. I also had to lie to my husband. I kept certain bills from him so he wouldn't find out. The lying tore me up inside."

Gloria explained that at first she tried to stop herself by not going to the stores. "I decided I would just stay home when I wasn't at work. Then I got addicted to Internet shopping. For instance, I decided to buy my eight-year-old nephew a birthday gift. I promised myself that I would spend only $30, no more. I found some little toy cars for sale—a few dollars each. Although I told myself I wouldn't spend more than $30, I ended up spending about $5000 on those little cars. I couldn't believe what I had done."

Although she regretted having spent so much on her nephew, Gloria told me that she was back on the Internet later that same day. "I bought four snowblowers and twenty black T-shirts. The odd thing is that we already had a snowblower and I don't wear T-shirts. Why would anyone do such a thing?" Over the next few months, Gloria began arriving late for work and then missing work. Instead, she was shopping on the Internet. "I would start shopping in the morning. After a while, I would look at the clock and realize that six or eight hours had passed and I had missed the entire workday." Even while at work, Gloria thought about items she'd like to purchase. Feeling these urges to shop also made it difficult for Gloria to concentrate — she started making mistakes. When Gloria did shop, however, she felt "peaceful": "It's not really happiness; instead, it's a relief, like some internal pressure that needs to come out. On the other hand, if something happens to keep me from shopping, I feel worse. This pressure builds up in my head, and in my whole body. I want to scream. Instead, I just become really irritable."

Gloria quit spending time with her husband, choosing to shop instead. Her marriage was suffering. "I love my husband, but the urges to shop were so strong—I couldn't resist. Also, I couldn't tell him about the shopping. I thought it was a major character flaw. How could he continue to love me once he knew how weak and undisciplined I was?"

Gloria lost her job, and the bills became too overwhelming to hide from her husband. "I remember the day I had to tell him about my problem. I had already spent all of our savings. I probably had $80,000 in credit card debt. I was so ashamed to tell him. I remember the look of betrayal on his face. I knew the marriage was over. I had lied to him and stolen from him. I hated myself."

Gloria's husband left her. Shortly thereafter, Gloria tried to overdose on aspirin and was admitted to a psychiatric hospital. She never told the doctors about the shopping problem; instead, she just told them she was depressed. "I never knew the shopping was an actual illness. I thought if I told the doctors, they wouldn't help me — it didn't seem like a medical problem. This is the first time I've told anyone other than my husband. This may be hard for you to believe, and it sounds silly, but shopping has ruined my family."

* * *

Compulsive shopping is a painful and yet virtually unknown mental illness. Most people who suffer from this problem, like Gloria, tell no one. Many do not even know it's an illness. Instead, they think they have no self-control. Also, rather than telling their physician and risking embarrassment, they report feeling depressed and keep the shopping problem secret.

Although many aspects of compulsive shopping remain a mystery, we do have treatments for this disorder. Gloria was successfully treated with a combination of medications, including an antidepressant (a selective serotonin reuptake inhibitor [SSRI]) and an atypical neuroleptic. Although she still occasionally has urges to shop, the urges are now mild, and she can easily resist them. Since treatments for compulsive shopping are available, physicians need to ask their patients and people need to tell their physicians when compulsive shopping is an issue.

Nancy: The Story of a Kleptomaniac (Compulsive Shoplifter)

I will never forget meeting Nancy, the first patient with kleptomania that I treated. As she walked into my office late one evening, I was struck by how nervous she was. Perspiration covered her forehead, her hands were trembling, and her voice quivered as she introduced herself. A fifty-two-year-old married woman, Nancy had gone to several psychiatrists before seeing me for what she described initially as depression and anxiety. At the interview, Nancy certainly was suffering from an anxious depression, but there also appeared to be something else she wasn't telling me.

After the initial interview, I received a letter from Nancy. In the letter, she referred to herself as the "devil's spawn." "I have been a horrible person for so long that I can't bring myself to tell you these things in person. I'm a thief. I steal something almost every day. You probably won't believe this, but I don't want the stuff I take.

I don't have any idea why I take the things I do. I have plenty of money. Most of the items I steal I don't want or need. That's why I'm depressed. How can I feel good when I'm such an evil person? If you don't want to treat me any longer, I'll understand."

I called Nancy immediately upon receiving this letter to tell her that I would like to continue treating her. I stressed that she had an illness and that it wasn't a character flaw. Although she was somewhat reluctant, Nancy agreed to come for another appointment.

"I was probably fourteen years old when I started stealing," she said. "I would go to stores with my mother. When I saw certain objects, I would get urges to steal them. The odd thing was that the items I stole were so ridiculous. I remember stealing key chains for several months, maybe three or four times a week. I didn't use them. I wasn't even sure why I stole them. Then I went several months where I stole batteries—hundreds of batteries. Every time I stole something, I felt a sort of 'rush.' The problem was that almost immediately after each theft, I felt guilty and ashamed. I wanted so much to tell my mother, but I couldn't. I was so afraid she'd quit loving me.

"When I got older, things got even worse. I continued to have urges to steal when I entered stores, but the items needed to be more expensive to make the urges go away. Also, I was having urges more often, and so I needed to steal more often. I couldn't steal just batteries anymore. Instead, I began to steal vacuums or lamps. One time I stole seven blenders at the same time. I remember just walking out with them in a cart. No one stopped me." Nancy admitted that as a well-dressed, attractive physician she had never been stopped by security when the alarms sounded. "By the time I reached thirty years of age, I was stealing about four to five times per week."

"How has this affected your life?" I asked.

"My entire life has been torment," she replied. "Each day I worry about having the urges, and then I worry about being caught stealing. I can't relax. Also, I was raised with morals, and I know what I'm doing is wrong. I'm a common criminal. Every night I go to bed hoping, praying that tomorrow will be different, that I won't want to steal anything. My prayers are never answered. I keep telling myself, 'just stop,' but I can't. I'm married with a sixteen-year-old daughter. I haven't even told my husband. He could never understand. I don't even understand. What if my daughter knew that her mother was a thief?"

Nancy had been apprehended only once, although she had been stealing for almost forty years. She was unable to look me in the eyes as she told the story of her apprehension. "I had stolen several things from a department store, including one expensive man's tie. Sometimes after I steal, I donate the items to the Salvation Army, throw them away, or give them away as gifts. On this particular evening I decided to give the tie to my husband. I hadn't stolen it with that intent. When I got home, I gave it to him, and he loved it. In fact, he put it on immediately. He was so happy, even though looking at it flooded me with guilt. I didn't know that there were cameras in the store. Shortly after I returned home, the police came to the door. I will never forget my husband's face as they took the tie off his neck. He just looked at me in horror as the police told him I had stolen it. I lied to him yet again when I told him I didn't do it." Nancy started crying. Her pain seemed too much to bear.

Nancy had gone to two psychiatrists over the last several years. Although she had told them about the stealing, they were unable to help. "Because they were unfamiliar with kleptomania, it was hard for them to understand my problem. I think they tried, but they didn't really get it. No one knew how badly I suffered. They tried to tell me to resist my impulse to steal or just try to stop. They saw the stealing as a minor oddity. They never seemed to get the idea that the stealing was why I was coming to see a psychiatrist." Instead, Nancy was treated for depression with an SSRI, which was helpful for her depression but not for her kleptomania. "I still have urges every day and cannot stop stealing."

Nancy had also gone to several support groups for people with various mental disorders such as depression. "I talked about my depression and my difficulties with my husband, but I couldn't discuss the stealing. How could they possibly understand? I was also afraid that they would reject me for being a criminal if they knew the truth. I guess I was just wasting my time—my fears kept me from getting help."

At the time I saw Nancy, she was considering suicide. "I can't go on stealing like this, and hating myself daily for doing so." Nancy had never been without her urges to steal. She simply could not imagine a life free from this burden. I recommended a new combination of medications—an opioid antagonist in addition to her antidepressant. Four weeks after starting the medication, Nancy came to the clinic. "I can't believe what I'm about to tell you. I quit stealing. These pills are miraculous. I still have urges to steal, but they're less intense and less frequent. It's a real triumph to be able to resist them." Nancy has been able to refrain from stealing for the last nine months.

Although it was first described in medical literature almost 200 years ago, kleptomania is one of the most poorly understood problems in psychiatry. For years there were debates about whether kleptomania was even an illness. Many thought it was merely criminal behavior. We now realize that kleptomania is a disabling illness.

Nancy's story is very typical of those we hear from people who suffer from kleptomania. These people often find it difficult to tell their families, their loved ones, or their physicians about their urges to steal. They hate themselves because of the stealing. People with kleptomania suffer the shame of engaging in criminal behavior and the frustration of being unable to stop this behavior.

Until recently, kleptomania was considered quite rare. It may, however, be more common than it has been thought to be. The prohibition against stealing is mentioned in the Ten Commandments as one of the ten moral precepts of Judeo-Christian thought. The shame associated with stealing prevents many people from discussing their problem. Even though more is now known about kleptomania, it continues to be an underrecognized disorder.

Gregg: The Story of a Sexually Compulsive Person

Gregg called me shortly after seeing me on a local news show where I was interviewed about compulsive gambling. Gregg, a thirty-seven-year-old married man who worked in advertising, was quick to inform me that he did not gamble. "When I was listening to you talk about gambling, I thought it sounded a lot like my problem. You mentioned how these gamblers can't stop their behavior, that they have these urges that are so intense, and I realized it's the same for me." Gregg was obviously hesitant to discuss his problem. "I have the same problem with sex. Is that a psychiatric problem, or am I just a pervert?" Gregg began to cry and hung up.

A couple of days later, Gregg called to schedule an appointment and came to the clinic. Noticeably shy and nervous, Gregg sat quietly for several minutes before he began talking. He apologized for hanging up. "I had never told that to anyone, and when I heard myself say it, I was so ashamed. Am I a sick person? I feel like some sort of degenerate." Gregg proceeded to tell his story. Although he had been married for fourteen years, Gregg often felt urges to have sex with strange women. "It's not really about seeking some thrill. Certain times I feel so tense and anxious, and then I feel these urges. The urges are uncontrollable. I know I shouldn't cheat on my wife— I love her—but I can't stop. After I have sex, I feel so calm. Of course, that quickly disappears as the guilt floods me."

Gregg's compulsive sexual behavior had started when he was about twenty-one. Getting married did not dampen the urges. "I have urges three or four times per week. I only act on the urges maybe one time every couple of weeks. I try to distract myself until the urges leave. They may last for a couple of hours, and during that time I'm a real bastard—irritable, angry, tense. I would have sex more often, but it's not easy to find women during the day to have sex with.

"These urges and behavior have ruined my life. I live each day with so much guilt and shame. And yet, given the opportunity, I would continue to have sex. Why do I continue doing something even when I see that it's destroying my life, my self-respect, and my marriage? You tell me I have a psychiatric illness, but I don't believe that. I'm a bad person, and no amount of medication or therapy is going to help me."

Although we had several meetings in which we discussed his compulsive sexual behavior and possible treatment options, Gregg eventually quit coming for treatment. At that time, he was still struggling with his symptoms and with the shame. Although there is no universally accepted definition of compulsive sexual behavior, it generally refers to sexual behavior that is excessive and that leads to difficulties (work-related or personal) in a person's life or to feelings of distress. Although there are some promising treatment options for this illness, embarrassment and shame often prevent people from seeking treatment.

Impulse Control Disorders in Children and Adolescents

If adults who suffer from impulse control disorders have difficulty talking about these problems because of embarrassment and shame, consider how difficult it must be for children and adolescents. The professional literature on these illnesses suggests that most of them start during late childhood or adolescence, and yet most physicians and family members are unfamiliar with them.

Betty was thirteen years old when she started stealing. At first her parents thought that she, like many children who steal, was doing it because she wanted something or because she was upset about something. However, Betty didn't know why she was stealing. Obviously embarrassed at having been brought to a psychiatrist and ashamed of what she had been doing, Betty was hesitant to talk. "I get these feelings to take things. They scare me because I know it's wrong and I know my parents will be upset, but I can't stop myself." Betty had been stealing softballs from the school. Her mother had found about fourteen softballs in the basement where Betty had hidden them. Betty did not play softball or ever use these balls. When asked why she took the softballs, Betty started to cry. "I don't know. Help me stop."

Some impulse control disorders do not show themselves until late adolescence. Because younger children usually do not have access to unlimited amounts of money, compulsive shopping and compulsive gambling may not become problems until adolescence. Steven was seventeen years old when his parents brought him to our clinic. He had started playing cards with some adults in the neighborhood on a daily basis. He had been staying out all night gambling, was failing school, was no longer dating, and had accumulated large financial debts to the other players, debts that he could not repay. Steven discussed his gambling like any of the adult patients we treat. "I'm thinking about it all day. I keep thinking of ways I can win and get my money back." When asked if he had urges or cravings to gamble, Steven replied, "I get an intense desire to play cards. If my parents try to stop me, I'll lie, run away, or do whatever I have to so I can play."

Sharon was sixteen years old when her mother brought her to an appointment. Having been raised in an affluent family, Sharon had her own credit card when she was fourteen. Her mother had become concerned about Sharon's shopping habits. Sharon often left school early to go to the mall alone to shop. She described having thoughts all day about various things she wanted to buy. Initially she went shopping with friends, but she had recently started to prefer going on her own. "I don't think of shopping as something I like to do anymore, so I don't want friends around. It's now something I have to do. If I don't buy something every day, I feel so tense."

Impulse control disorders usually start in adolescence, but children may also suffer from these disorders. Although we do not know how common these problems are in children or adolescents, people may be particularly vulnerable to the development of these disorders during adolescence. Adults whom we treat usually tell us that their behaviors began, at least to some degree, during their teen years. Also, these disorders start gradually in most people, and so they may first appear in childhood or adolescence but not become a problem until later in life.

Living with Behavioral Addicts: Stories of Family Members

Having been featured on television and in newspapers, we have received letters and emails from all over the world from people who are concerned about family members and loved ones. Sometimes the person writing us wonders if a family member has an impulse control disorder, and other times he or she is asking for treatment recommendations.

One man in Australia wrote us about his son. "My son is twenty-five years old, and I am trying to figure out if he is a kleptomaniac. He has been stealing for eight years and has been in prison twice. My wife and I had pretty much given up on him. After reading your story about kleptomania, we started to wonder if he had it. I'm not trying to make excuses for my son, but he has stolen some very peculiar items over the years. If he has an illness, I need to get help for him. If he had a heart problem, I wouldn't let that go untreated."

Many family members feel helpless as they watch a loved one continue with self-destructive behavior. The sense of isolation and shame that the patient feels is often felt by members of his or her family as well. A woman from Ireland wrote the following email about her daughter: "I watched my daughter ruin her life, the lives of her husband and children, and I could do nothing. My daughter, I believe, suffered from compulsive shopping. She was out of control—spending everything she and her husband made. They lost everything. She then went into a severe depression and took her own life. I watched this for about two years and did nothing. I didn't know it was an illness. Instead, I criticized her for being so irresponsible.

I was so ashamed of what others might think of her, and of me. I never tried to get her into treatment. In fact, I quit talking to her because she always wanted to borrow money. I blame myself for her death."

Another mother called to tell us about her daughter. "I just watch her gamble her life away. She's a smart young woman, and she is destroying herself. I feel that I must have done something to cause this. Or at the very least that I should be able to stop her. I'm her mother, I love her, and all I can do is sit and watch. I have never felt such pain."

The fact that these disorders can be treated effectively is highlighted by the following note we received from the wife of a pathological gambler. "My husband's illness has been so devastating for so long. He started gambling when he retired. Almost immediately he had a problem. He was never home. He spent all of his time at the casino. We lost our retirement savings. We had to ask our children for financial help. That was so humiliating. We should be helping them, not the other way around. It also hurt our relationships with our children. I didn't think they wanted us to call anymore because they feared we wanted money. My husband and I spent evenings crying, with him promising not to gamble anymore. Those moments were short-lived, however, and he would be back to the casino in a couple of days. Anyhow, once we realized that this was an illness, we looked for a psychiatrist. Finally, after a dozen attempts, we found someone who felt comfortable treating compulsive gambling. My husband is probably 75 percent better, and we are starting to rebuild our lives and our relationships with our children."

Common Secrets

Data on impulse control disorders are incomplete. These disorders, however, may affect a substantial number of people. Estimates of the possible prevalence of these disorders in the U.S. population suggest that each impulse control disorder may be far more common than was previously thought: pathological gambling, 1 to 5 percent of the population; kleptomania, 0.5 to 1 percent; compulsive shopping, 1.8 to 5 percent; and compulsive sexual behavior, 5 percent. Most of these estimates, however, are derived from studies of various specific populations, such as college students or patients at certain medical clinics. Whether the illnesses are more or less common than these estimates is still unclear at this time, but the numbers suggest that these are not rare problems.

Impulse control disorders have many things in common: People are engaging in behaviors that they cannot resist; they usually have urges to perform these behaviors; the urges and behaviors cause emotional distress and interfere with their day-to-day functioning. Some people try to resist the urges, with varying degrees of success. Others are overwhelmed and may engage in the behavior almost automatically. Regardless of their degree of control over their behavior, patients suffering from impulse control disorders all feel shame because of their behavior. The shame and the secrecy the behavior engenders appear to be inherent in these disorders and are probably the first and sometimes greatest enemies to overcome.

Overcoming the secrecy and shame is an important first step in seeking treatment, and there is preliminary evidence that psychiatric treatment is often beneficial for these disorders. Several medications and certain forms of psychotherapy have shown promise in alleviating the symptoms of these illnesses. Although there is much that we still don't know about these disabling and distressing illnesses, we can offer hope to those who suffer from them.

2

What Are Impulse Control Disorders?

Impulse control disorders occupy a unique place among psychiatric disorders. Mental health professionals in the United States and in many other countries use diagnostic criteria set forth in the DSM-IV (*Diagnostic and Statistical Manual*, fourth edition) to make psychiatric diagnoses. These criteria identify the basic features of a disorder, symptoms that everyone with that disorder experiences. Pathological gambling has detailed criteria, and kleptomania has skeletal criteria. Although there are no universally accepted criteria for compulsive shopping and compulsive sexual behavior, there are certain generally agreed upon guidelines for diagnosing these other disorders.

The definition of pathological gambling involves a persistent and maladaptive pattern of gambling behavior that includes five or more of these symptoms:

1. Preoccupied with gambling
2. Needs to use increasing amounts of money to achieve desired excitement
3. Repeated unsuccessful efforts to control, cut back, or stop gambling
4. Restless or irritable when attempting to cut down or stop
5. Gambles to escape problems or relieve dysphoric mood
6. After losing, returns to get even ("chases" losses)
7. Lies to family, therapist, or others
8. Has committed illegal acts to finance gambling
9. Has jeopardized or lost a significant relationship, job, or opportunity because of gambling
10. Relies on others to provide money or relieve a desperate situation caused by gambling

People with pathological gambling don't just have an occasional thought about gambling—they are preoccupied with it. Some pathological gamblers find it difficult not to think about gambling: "I'm thinking about gambling all day at work." "I don't seem to be able to concentrate because gambling is always on my mind." "I'm obsessed with gambling." People with pathological gambling tend to spend at least one hour every day thinking about gambling.

The definition of pathological gambling also describes how the gambling affects people's lives—lying, illegal acts, jeopardizing work and social relationships. These criteria, along with attempts to cut down or quit, may make readers think of alcoholics. In fact, the criteria for pathological gambling were borrowed from the criteria used to describe alcohol dependence.

These criteria reflect the impairment of pathological gamblers and help guard against overdiagnosis. Not everyone who gambles, or even everyone who is preoccupied with gambling, suffers from pathological gambling. After all, gambling is very common, and *preoccupation* can be a very subjective term. Therefore, the requirement that several objective measures of impairment are necessary to make the diagnosis attempts to draw a line between normal and excessive behavior. The distinction between normal gambling and excessive or pathological gambling, however, is often not quite clear. What if someone meets four rather than the required five criteria? Where normal gambling leaves off and pathological gambling begins is sometimes a difficult judgment call. In the case of moderate to severe gambling behavior—like Robert's—the impairment is significant, and the diagnosis clearly applies.

Like pathological gambling, kleptomania is best characterized as an inability to resist an urge. In the case of kleptomania, that urge is to steal objects, often objects that are not needed for personal use or that are not desired for their monetary value. People with kleptomania often feel a sense of tension or anxiety immediately before stealing something. They also may feel pleasure, relief of anxiety or tension, or gratification at the time of the actual theft. In cases of kleptomania, there is also the same shame and secrecy seen with pathological gamblers.

The criterion that people with kleptomania have an inability to resist an impulse to steal is the primary way in which kleptomania is differentiated from shoplifting. Shoplifters steal for a variety of reasons—they want something, they want something they can sell for money, they're angry with the store, etc. Kleptomaniacs steal because they cannot resist the urge to steal.

The complication in the diagnosis is the phrase "objects that are not needed for personal use or desired for their monetary value." We have several patients who report that although they originally stole items that fit this criterion, they may also steal things that they need. As one woman reported, "I get these urges to steal something. When I first started stealing, I took a lot of senseless items, things I definitely didn't need or want. Over time, however, I realized that if I'm putting myself on the line to satisfy an urge, why not take something I can use?"

Shopping is considered compulsive if the patient describes frequent preoccupation with shopping or with urges to shop. Additionally, the person may shop more frequently than he or she can afford, frequently buy unnecessary items, or shop for longer periods of time than intended. In addition, compulsive shopping requires that the thoughts, the urges, or the shopping itself cause marked distress, be time-consuming, significantly interfere with social or occupational functioning, or result in financial problems.

As with pathological gambling, the requirement of distress or impairment prevents everyone who believes he or she shops too much from being diagnosed as a compulsive shopper. In the United States, where credit card debt is a large problem and people often shop beyond their means, the line between normal behavior and excessive shopping is often blurred. This distinction is further obscured by messages from magazines, television, and movies that amplify the desire to shop by suggesting that certain items are necessary if one is to be beautiful or happy. How much distress is required for the diagnosis? How much impairment?

Compulsive shopping is not the same as impulse buying. The latter term refers to people who buy things in the grocery line that they don't really need. Impulse buying seems to be triggered by marketing strategies that determine the types of items that will entice people and then place those items where they can be easily chosen. There is currently no evidence that people who "impulse buy" have commonalities with people who shop compulsively.

Compulsive sexual behavior involves excessive or uncontrolled behavior or sexual urges or thoughts that lead to subjective distress, social or occupational impairment, or legal and financial consequences. There may be an element of anxiety reduction as a factor motivating compulsive sexual behavior and a failure to control one's sexual behavior despite significant harmful consequences.

These disorders have the core common feature of urges. Although the term *urge* is not included in the definition of any of the illnesses, patients report the behavior as being secondary to cravings or urges to perform the act. The idea of urges is actually implied by labeling these disorders *impulse* control disorders, but the word *urge* has been avoided because of the difficulty in defining an urge. Urges are not the same as "wanting" to perform some act. Patients who have urges to perform these activities can clearly discuss the urges they have.

Pathological gambling and kleptomania are diagnosed by the criteria set forth in the DSM-IV. Although the absence of some impulse control disorders from the DSM-IV is a limitation of the manual, the DSM-IV criteria are beneficial because they provide a common language for patients and clinicians. It's important that when we refer to "pathological gambling," every clinician conjures up the same idea, regardless of where he or she practices. Thus, the criteria provide uniformity in diagnosis. The criteria also provide knowledge for people suffering from these disorders: "I didn't know that what I had been doing for years had a name. That came as a relief to me." The DSM-IV criteria, however, do not tell us about these people's lives, their difficulties with others, the isolation they experience, or the shame and embarrassment they feel. Several people can meet the criteria for a disorder and can have aspects of the illness in common, but the experiences each of them has because of the illness are unique.

Levels of Severity

Sandra, a thirty-two-year-old nurse, called to schedule an appointment, "I don't think I have a problem with shopping, but my husband is worried about me. He wants me to see you. I may shop a lot, but I don't think it's a psychiatric problem. I'm not even sure I should waste your time."

Sandra came to the appointment with her husband one evening after work. We talked about her work at a nearby hospital. She had been at the same job for nearly ten years and had never had a problem with attendance, with peers, or with patients. By all accounts, Sandra was doing very well in her job, and she enjoyed her work: "I really enjoy what I do." At this point in the interview, I was unclear about why Sandra had come to see me.

"I guess the problem is with my relationships outside of work. I admit I shop a lot more than I used to. I'm not sure why. We've never had much money, and so I really never spent much time in stores. During the last six or eight months I've started shopping a lot more. The problem is that I don't really want or need the things I buy—it sounds crazy. I just buy things for the heck of it. The other day I went to buy our six-year-old daughter a pair of school shoes. I think I purchased $200 or $300 worth of clothing for her, and I bought a few things for my husband as well—again I spent a few hundred dollars. My daughter and husband didn't need the things I bought. The credit card bills are starting to add up."

"Other than the credit card debt, does your shopping cause you problems?" I asked.

"I think it's taking a toll on my marriage," she answered. "I don't always tell him about some of the things I buy or how much they cost. When he finds out, he feels like I've been hiding things from him, and I guess he's right. I do feel that for the first time in our marriage I'm hiding things from my husband. I just know he'll be angry, and so why tell him. It's not as if I know why I'm buying these things—I don't have good reasons for the purchases, and so I have nothing to tell him."

Sandra's husband, David, who had been sitting quietly during the interview, suddenly interrupted. "I think we're having problems because shopping is all she wants to do. She sits and reads catalogues all day when she's not at work. I ask her to do something with the kids and she takes them shopping. I don't think she can enjoy herself unless she's shopping. I don't think she likes to do things with me anymore. Don't get me wrong, Sandra's a great wife and mother, but this shopping is getting out of hand. She's not even interested in what our daughters are doing at school. I love my wife, but I'm starting to think that all she loves is buying things."

Sandra looked noticeably upset. "I love my husband and my daughter, more than anything. But I'm so preoccupied with buying things—and that's all they are, things. I don't know why, but I do think about shopping a large part of the day. I watch television, or look at magazines or catalogues, and I get these urges to shop. I wish I could be more involved with my family, but part of my mind is somewhere else."

I asked Sandra if there were other factors that might be contributing to the problems at home. "I've been asking myself that question for months. Am I just unhappy and trying to buy happiness with objects? I don't think so. I don't feel depressed. I don't cry or feel hopeless about my life. David and I have had problems, as any married couple does, but I enjoy my life and love my family. When I was younger, I would shop when I had bad days at school or work. But I would buy myself something I wanted. I'm not buying myself things like that. Now, I just buy anything."

It did sound as if Sandra suffered from compulsive shopping. She was distressed because of her preoccupations, she had urges to shop, and her relationships had suffered because of her urges. I wondered how she managed to function so well at work. "At work, I'm constantly on the go. I don't have time to think about shopping, or anything else, for that matter. When I do have down time, however, I guess thoughts of shopping do enter my head. It just seems easier to distract myself at work."

Most people who suffer from compulsive shopping, or the other impulse control disorders, don't like to admit the difficulty their symptoms cause them. Many try to ignore the urges and thoughts and go on with their jobs, with their duties at home, and with their lives. But even when the symptoms are relatively mild, it is usually a struggle to do so. "I'm a nurse and I see people every day with real problems. Here I am talking about shopping, and I feel guilty even thinking of this in the same way. Even though I know it's not so bad, it still bothers me."

Rebecca had scheduled an appointment in our clinic without indicating what her problem was. On the day of the appointment, an elegantly dressed sixty-three-year-old woman entered the clinic with her husband. When she was seated in my office, she began, "I'm not sure I need to be here. I would like you to tell me if I have a problem. My husband apparently believes I'm crazy or something."

"Why would he think that?" I asked, having no idea what problem she might be struggling with.

"I like to play the slot machines," she stated with only a hint of embarrassment.

"It started a few years ago. When the casinos opened, I thought it might be fun to go for an evening. My husband and I went together. The slot machines were my favorite game. I didn't have to interact with others. I could just sit there and play the game without too many distractions. Since that time, my husband and I go fairly regularly—perhaps once a week. I know people who go much more often than we do and have severe financial problems because of it. We have no financial difficulties. In fact, I'm not sure the gambling has caused any problems for us."

Not exactly sure why Rebecca was in my office, I turned to her husband for clarification. "She has a problem," he asserted. "Sure, we probably go to the casino only one night a week, but she'd go more often if I didn't stop her. I don't even like going to the casino, but she pleads with me until I give in. The slot machines are all she talks about—how much time she spent on one machine, whether she should have switched machines, etc. She used to have interests— she'd work in the garden, have coffee with friends, or go shopping with our oldest daughter and her child. She has given all that up. I feel like I have to go with her or she'd never come home. You don't know what she's like when she wants to go—she's becomes so unpleasant. I swear she's changed. She's right that her gambling hasn't caused us financial problems, but she has been spending more money at the casino. Sometimes I wish we were broke—maybe that would stop her."

Rebecca had sat quietly, listening to her husband. "I know it bothers him. I've tried to quit, but I just can't. I enjoy playing the slot machines. I don't enjoy what it's done to my marriage, though. I'm not sure I'm quite as obsessed with it as he suggests, but I do think about it probably too much.

"Gambling reminds me of when I used to smoke. That same sort of craving comes over me. When that happens, I need to go to the casino. I know my friends are upset with me—I never seem to have time to do things with them. The truth is that I prefer to gamble. It makes me feel energized or excited or something. I didn't think it was a problem because we aren't having the financial difficulties that you hear gambling addicts have."

Ethan was a nineteen-year-old university student who came to my office asking for help because of his stealing. It is rare for me to see cases of kleptomania among late adolescents or young adults. Most people who suffer from kleptomania feel intense shame. They usually steal for years before they ask for psychiatric help, if they ask at all. The only young people I usually see are those I am asked to see by the courts, and in most of those cases the person is simply a thief hoping for leniency by claiming to have a mental illness. When I was told that Ethan had not been sent by anyone, I was initially skeptical.

"I'm not sure I'm in the right place. I was told you help people with kleptomania."

"What do you know about kleptomania?" I asked.

"I know it's when you cannot stop yourself from stealing," he replied. "You also steal stupid things. That's why I think I have it. I've been stealing things for years, ever since I was a little kid. At first I would take things from stores—you know, candy, baseball cards, and stuff. Now I steal things that don't make sense. Yesterday I took several cans of insect spray from the hardware store. I don't know why. I didn't need it. I don't steal all that often—maybe once every couple of months—but it still bothers me a lot. Usually I think about it and then just put it out of my mind. Other times I just can't stop myself."

"Has the stealing caused problems for you?" I asked.

"I'm not really sure," he replied. "I haven't gotten caught or had legal problems. I think it has caused some difficulties with my girlfriend. She doesn't know I steal, but not telling her makes me feel guilty, and I think I act differently because of it. I guess the real problem is that I feel there's something about me that I don't have complete control over."

Like Sandra, Rebecca, and Ethan, most people with impulse control disorders have a torturous relationship with their behavior.

On the one hand, the activity of shopping or gambling brings either joy or relief from anxiety-provoking urges or thoughts. On the other hand, the thoughts and urges distract these people from other areas of their lives, and the behavior itself causes personal, social, or occupational problems. Even mild cases of impulse control disorders can be emotionally distressing and can interfere with a person's social life or work.

Impulse control disorders span a spectrum of severity. Whereas Sandra, Rebecca, and Ethan had milder forms of compulsive shopping, pathological gambling, and kleptomania, Gloria, Robert, and Nancy had severe forms. When impulse control disorders are severe, they can significantly affect most aspects of people's lives—work, social, and personal. Some people lose their jobs, their marriages, and their friends. They may become so ashamed of their problem that they stop communicating with friends and family, stay locked up in their homes, and consider and even commit suicide.

Most people with these disorders, however, do not become socially isolated or end up taking their lives. Instead, like Sandra, Rebecca, and Ethan, those with milder cases of impulse control disorders usually describe relatively normal lives, although with some impairment. These people have jobs, are in relationships, and raise families. In fact, many of our patients have very good jobs and are quite productive. Although these people with milder cases of impulse control disorders suffer, what they describe is usually decreased productivity or quality of life, not devastation.

Impulse control disorders vary in severity from person to person. These disorders may also vary in other ways. Some pathological gamblers play only the slot machines; others play only blackjack. Some have urges that are triggered by sensory stimuli (e.g., billboards); others have cravings only when they feel stressed. Some compulsive shoppers buy only from one store, while others shop at multiple places. Some kleptomaniacs steal only from grocery stores, whereas others might steal only from friends and clothing stores.

Even though all people with impulse control disorders have certain things in common, no two people with the same impulse control disorder have exactly the same experience. Severity, presentation, feelings associated with the behavior, and related difficulties (family, legal, or work) may all differ. Everyone with an impulse control disorder has an urge to engage in a certain behavior that she or he knows is not in her or his best interest. Everyone with such a disorder also has thoughts about the behavior—is preoccupied with it. Everyone with such a disorder is distressed by the thoughts, urges, or behavior, or doesn't function well because of them. However, the specific details of how the impulse control disorder presents differ from person to person.

What Impulse Control Disorders Are Not

Few illnesses provoke the sense of frustration and self-hatred that impulse control disorders do. Many people who suffer from these disorders repeatedly engage in behavior that they regret and are ashamed of—stealing, sex, gambling, and uncontrollable shopping. "I must be a truly evil person if I can continue to steal and not stop myself," stated George, a thirty-four-year-old married man who suffered from kleptomania. Twila, a fifty-six-year-old divorced pathological gambler, described herself as the "lowest life form" when she forged checks to pay for her gambling debt. Marsha, a forty-three-year-old mother of two, cried as she described stealing money from her children's piggy banks to go gambling: "What sort of wicked mother am I?" And Michael, a twenty-seven-year-old married man who suffered from compulsive sexual behavior, was adamant when he stated, "I don't deserve to live."

Although the indications that patients with impulse control disorders have something wrong with their brains are numerous, strong, and too important to ignore, most people who suffer from these illnesses have difficulty believing that their problems are anything but bad behavior, poor character, or lack of willpower. Has a person lost his or her "free will" when he or she performs some action that he or she finds shameful and doesn't want to do? In no other disorder do patients stress the importance of willpower when describing their behavior: "I want to stop stealing, but when I have urges I can't resist them." "I don't plan on gambling, but then I start having these cravings to go to the casino. If I weren't so weak, I could probably quit." "I think it's sick that I'm looking for sex all day—I desperately want to stop, but I just can't." What complicates this picture is that patients also tell us that they can often stop their behavior for periods of time if they exert "enough willpower." Of course, when the behavior resumes, they feel that they have become "weak" or "lazy."

Other people live in torment because they believe that their urges are "bad," "immoral," or "evil." One patient who suffered from kleptomania told us, "Good people don't have urges like these. I feel like I must be a bad person if I can think such thoughts." A young woman who suffered from compulsive sexual behavior said, "Every time I have thoughts or cravings to engage in sexual behavior, I think I should just kill myself and rid the world of me."

Many physicians and psychiatrists unfortunately do not ask patients about these disorders, and may not accept these illnesses as "real" psychiatric problems. Patients often tell us that when they discussed these behaviors, previous physicians had simply told them to "stop doing that." This response by poorly informed health-care professionals simply compounds the shame that these people feel and may in fact prevent people from seeking further assistance for these problems.

Impulse control disorders are not a result of being a bad person, having a bad character, or being weak-willed. There is a brain physiology that gives rise to these problems. These illnesses are probably caused by an abnormal processing of pleasure and reward signals within the brain. Because these people have problems with "will" and with "urges," philosophers have historically considered these issues more than physicians have. "Urges" and "willpower," however, have now become words used in medical circles. As we discuss later, new discoveries about these illnesses may reveal the biology of the mind at a level never considered possible.

3

Who Has an Impulse Control Disorder?

Shame and Secrecy

Are you ashamed of some behavior that you currently engage in? Is there some behavior you perform that you keep secret from friends or loved ones? Affirmative answers to these questions may suggest an inability to control the behavior. Shame and secrecy are fundamental to impulse control disorders. The shame and secrecy often prevent physicians from making the proper diagnosis because people will not discuss their symptoms with others. This is the case even with people who have been under the care of a psychiatrist. They will often discuss feeling depressed, "out of control," and anxious, and might report financial difficulties or guilt, but they do not mention the specific behaviors of impulse control disorders. Because of the shame and secrecy, care providers need to ask patients about these problems. Very few patients who suffer from these disorders will raise the issue on their own.

There are several reasons for the shame and secrecy. People are afraid to mention many of these behaviors because there may be legal consequences. People with kleptomania fear arrest for thefts. Disclosing compulsive sexual behavior may lead to divorce proceedings. People with pathological gambling and compulsive shopping often resort to illegal actions (forging checks, stealing, prostitution) to pay the debt resulting from their behavior. These disorders appear to be chronic illnesses, with the behavior often increasing in frequency and intensity if the disorder is left untreated. Although legal fears prevent people from disclosing these problems, the chance of correcting the behavior without assistance appears to be slight.

Another reason people refuse to talk about these illnesses is a fear that others will look down on them and judge them for being "weak" or "self-indulgent." One woman who stole said, "My family thinks I have no willpower and criticizes me constantly. Why would a doctor be any more understanding?" A psychiatrist who saw a person suffering from compulsive shopping had told the person, "You have to stop that." The psychiatrist, however, had failed to offer suggestions on how to accomplish this goal.

To complicate matters, people with impulse control disorders not only suffer from their symptoms, but also are the perpetrators of their distressing behavior. This may result in a person's being reluctant to pursue treatment. Even though these people may feel like victims of their illness, seeking help may be difficult for them, given their awareness of their role in the problem. Many also fear that they will be viewed like patients who engage in other "self-indulgent" behavior such as alcoholism or drug abuse.

A third reason people do not mention their impulse control behavior may be fear that the care provider will refuse to treat them for depression or anxiety once the "bad behavior" is mentioned. People with impulse control disorders may feel that they are responsible for ruining their lives, and they may worry that professionals will likewise blame them for their behavior. Unfortunately, many healthcare providers do in fact refuse to treat these disorders. This is particularly true in the case of kleptomania; many physicians simply see it as criminal behavior and believe that the criminal justice system is the proper avenue for correcting the behavior. In one case, after treating a woman for depression for several months, a psychiatrist found out that his female patient also suffered from compulsive sexual behavior. "That's immoral. If you want me to continue to treat your depression, you have to quit this sexual behavior. If you want to stop it, you can," he had informed her. Feeling judged by the physician, the woman stopped seeing him and stopped taking her antidepressants. Shortly thereafter she was admitted to a psychiatric hospital for a suicide attempt.

And finally, many people with impulse control disorders choose not to mention these problems to their physicians because they believe they can stop the behaviors if they try hard enough. Many of them feel that asking their physician for help is an admission that they have a problem they cannot fix on their own. Many people can in fact resist the urges to perform these various behaviors, but only for a short time. A few months appears to be the average length of time most people can resist the urges. One kleptomania patient who was in prison for theft was hoping that the incarceration would eliminate the urges to steal. After approximately six weeks, he started stealing from other inmates. A pathological gambler moved to a state that had no legal gambling in the hopes of resisting the urges to gamble. He started taking weekend vacations to Las Vegas after only two months in his new home.

Failure to Diagnose

Impulse control disorders may be more common than is generally thought. Pathological gambling and compulsive shopping are actually quite common (affecting perhaps 3 to 10 percent of the population). Although kleptomania and compulsive sexual behavior are not rare, the prevalence of these disorders has not been well studied. Even with conservative estimates, however, these disorders may also have lifetime prevalence rates of 0.5 to 5 percent respectively. When all of these percentages are translated into actual numbers, we see that perhaps 25 to 38 million Americans suffer from an impulse control disorder at some time in their lives. If these disorders are so common, however, why have most mental health workers seen few, if any, of these patients?

There are several possible explanations for this apparent discrepancy between the high estimated rates of impulse control disorders and the lack of these patients in psychiatric settings. As we have mentioned, shame may lead many people to keep their symptoms a secret. Additionally, many people who suffer from impulse control disorders do not know that their behavior constitutes a psychiatric illness. Most of them believe that they are engaging in immoral or illegal behavior and that they should be able to stop. They are unaware that these disorders have a biological basis in the brain and that psychiatric treatment is often effective. Instead, they may see their clergy or their primary physician. They often seek help for depression, which may be secondary to their inability to control their behavior. Very few health-care professionals know that the impulse control disorders are psychiatric illnesses with available treatments. Pathological gambling is possibly an exception to this lack of knowledge. Even in the case of pathological gambling, however, many physicians may not know where someone should go for treatment. Although these disorders have long histories in the medical literature, most family practitioners and many psychiatrists are unable to diagnose them. Believing them to be quite rare, physicians may never ask their patients questions about these possible problems.

Misdiagnosis

Impulse control disorders are often accompanied by depression or substance abuse, and many people choose to discuss these problems with their physicians instead of the impulse control disorders. Thus, people may receive diagnoses of depression or alcohol abuse instead of kleptomania or compulsive shopping. Also, even when people reveal the symptoms of impulse control disorders, some of them are told that the symptoms are merely a result of a deeper underlying problem. For instance, pathological gamblers are often told that the gambling is probably due to their feeling depressed or to difficulties at work. People with compulsive sexual behavior may be told that the behavior is secondary to relationship problems. A physician may tell someone with kleptomania that the stealing is merely an expression of her anxiety. In fact, impulse control disorders may coexist with these other problems. However, impulse control disorders should also be diagnosed and treated.

Impulse control disorders may produce symptoms that are very similar to those seen in other psychiatric disorders, such as obsessive-compulsive disorder or manic depression. The following are some of the disorders that often look like impulse control disorders.

Manic-depressive illness (bipolar disorder). Manic-depressive illness is defined as having episodes of depression and of mania (periods of time when a person feels hyper or euphoric, with impulsive or risky behavior, racing thoughts, and pressured speech). When people who have bipolar disorder are experiencing a manic episode, they may gamble with money they don't have, buy excessive amounts of things they don't need, steal things, and engage in risky sexual behavior. A manic episode may look like most of the impulse control disorders, and people with impulse control disorders may thus be misdiagnosed as having bipolar disorder. People with bipolar disorder, however, also have other symptoms that suggest that their mood is out of control — they aren't sleeping, they have an excessive number of goals or projects, and they have more energy than usual. In addition, manic episodes, if left untreated, may last only a few weeks. People with impulse control disorders report behavior of several months' or years' duration. Of course, it is possible to have both bipolar disorder and an impulse control disorder, in which case both diagnoses are appropriate.

Obsessive-compulsive disorder (OCD). OCD is defined by obsessions (recurrent, intrusive thoughts that disturb the person) and compulsions (repetitive behaviors intended to reduce the anxiety the obsessions cause). People who suffer from OCD have almost constant thoughts that keep coming into their minds. They perform certain rituals to stop these thoughts—they may make lists, clean or check things repeatedly, and say certain phrases over and over again. Many people with impulse control disorders may describe their problems in similar words: "I think about gambling all day." "I'm obsessed with shopping." "My sexual behavior is an obsession with me." "When I go into a store, all I think about is stealing something." Many people with impulse control disorders are therefore misdiagnosed as having OCD because of the preoccupation seen in impulse control disorders and the repetitive nature of the behaviors associated with these disorders. However, although these disorders have preoccupation with behavior in common with OCD, the behaviors associated with these disorders are generally ego-syntonic and rewarding. Compulsive behavior in OCD is ego-dystonic and performed as a way of alleviating anxiety. When a person reports uncontrollable urges to gamble, have sex, shop, or steal, an impulse control disorder should be diagnosed.

Major depressive disorder (depression). Depression refers to an individual experiencing a depressed mood or loss of interest or pleasure. In addition, the person may have weight loss, sleep changes, agitation, loss of energy, feelings of worthlessness, and concentration problems. Many people with impulse control disorders (perhaps 30 to 50 percent) also suffer from depression. For many, the mood is a result of the experience of gambling, stealing, etc. Alternatively, depression may bring out the impulse behavior in some people. For example, many female gamblers report that feeling depressed often results in urges to gamble. Patients with impulse control disorders, like those with alcohol or drug problems, may also find that the behavior helps them feel less depressed. Kleptomaniacs, gamblers, shoppers, and people with compulsive sexual urges may get a "high" from their behavior that alleviates a depressed mood. Another possibility is that certain people may be vulnerable to both problems. Because many people who suffer from impulse control disorders go to a physician when they feel depressed, they may be diagnosed with depression and never asked about their behavior. Because of shame, the person generally will not want to volunteer information about his or her behavior, and thus the actual problem may never be addressed.

Borderline personality disorder. A personality disorder means that a person has a set of enduring traits that lead to recurrent subjective distress or very impaired functioning. The traits that make up borderline personality disorder involve marked instability of self-image, mood, impulses, and relationships. People who suffer from this problem often look like people with an impulse control disorder because they may steal objects, engage in impulsive sexual acts, spend money recklessly, and gamble. Unlike people with impulse control disorders, however, people with borderline personality disorder also are easily upset, are unable to handle stable relationships, and have impaired abilities to handle adult responsibilities. People with impulse control disorders generally have stable relationships; they are often married and have families. These relationships suffer only when the addictive behaviors become severe or distract the person from familial responsibilities. In contrast, people with borderline personality disorder have unstable relationships throughout their lives.

Substance use disorders. Substance use disorders involve a maladaptive pattern of use that leads to significant impairment or distress. Some people with impulse control disorders abuse substances as a result of their impulse control disorder. They are upset about their behavior and respond to this by "escaping" from the problem by using substances. In fact, up to 50 percent of the impulse control disorder patients that we treat have had a substance use problem at some point in the past. Consequently, these people are often diagnosed with a substance use disorder, while the impulse control disorder is ignored or thought of as secondary to the substance use problem. Unfortunately, sometimes the impulse control disorder is the cause of the substance use problem, and therefore it is important to ask those with substance use problems whether there is anything that consistently triggers their use behavior.

Although impulse control disorders may often occur in a person who also has another problem, it is important that the impulse control disorder be diagnosed and treated. Other disorders may be diagnosed because patients are too ashamed to talk about the behavior associated with the impulse control disorder. When the physician asks about these problems in a nonjudgmental manner and listens to the response, impulse control disorders are usually fairly easy to recognize.

Common Characteristics

Men and women of any age may develop an impulse control disorder. Females appear to be at greater risk for developing kleptomania and compulsive shopping. The support for this statement, however, is only a few medication and phenomenological studies with small numbers of subjects. While we see more females seeking treatment for these disorders in our clinic, we also care for a large number of males with these problems.

In fact, there has been speculation that kleptomania and compulsive shopping may be more common in men than was previously thought. Men may simply be less likely to seek treatment for these problems. In the case of kleptomania, it may be the criminal justice system, not psychiatry, that deals with males with this disorder. Furthermore, in the case of compulsive shopping, men's generally greater incomes may delay early, more mild cases from coming to the attention of the mental health system. Thus, although men are underrepresented among those being treated for these disorders, they may suffer from these problems more than is often believed.

When Marc first came to our clinic, he was depressed about his finances. Marc suffered from compulsive shopping. At thirty-two years old, Marc had been wrestling with his shopping habits since his early twenties. It was in the last two years, however, that his buying became "out of control." A typical day for Marc involved going to work at the hospital, where he was employed in the accounting office. He would spend his free time on the Internet buying various items, none of which he really wanted or needed (one day he spent $700 on sheets for his home; another day he purchased $400 worth of pet supplies). He regretted his behavior once the purchases were made, but he felt he couldn't control the urge to buy the items. With credit card debt that was currently beyond his ability to repay, Marc was thinking about bankruptcy. Because his shopping had caused problems at work (difficulty concentrating during work, making foolish errors), he decided to take a leave of absence from the hospital. Because of the shame, he considered suicide. Independent of his shopping problem, Marc had also suffered from kleptomania (he stole from friends and from stores) since adolescence, with frequent exacerbations and remissions of stealing behavior. As the stress of his shopping increased, Marc found that he was stealing more regularly, often leading him to hoard numerous items he did not want.

The added difficulty for Marc was that he had read that both compulsive shopping and kleptomania were more common in females. Marc began to feel emasculated and worried that these problems reflected issues involving his gender or his sexuality. Although both problems had been ongoing for years, Marc had never told his doctor because of the shame of having a "women's disease." Part of Marc's treatment, therefore, involved education about these disorders. He was reassured that although these problems may be more common in females, they also occur in males and may affect millions of males all over the world.

Pathological gambling, unlike the other impulse control disorders, may be more common in males. This much-publicized finding, however, is based upon only a few epidemiological surveys and may not be the whole story. Although some studies indicate that twice as many males as females suffer from pathological gambling disorder, in our clinic we actually treat more women than men for pathological gambling. This may merely reflect women's willingness to seek treatment, or it may suggest that women with this problem tend to have a more severe form of the illness and therefore seek treatment. On the other hand, compulsive sexual behavior appears to be more common in men, and this may be due to men's greater willingness to seek help for this particular disorder.

There is still too little information available to say what the exact percentages of males and females with each disorder are. What we do know, however, is that both men and women suffer from these illnesses. There are differences between the genders with respect to these disorders (as we discuss in detail later), but there does not appear to be a difference in response to available treatment.

Impulse control disorders may affect people of all ages. These disorders have been observed both in children and in adults as late as their seventh decade. Studies have been fairly consistent in showing, however, that in most cases the behaviors associated with these problems start in early or late adolescence. Even though the behaviors start at this age, most people do not report symptoms consistent with the actual psychiatric disorders until several years later. For example, someone may start shopping at age fourteen but not report uncontrollable urges to shop until several years later. In fact, most of these disorders appear to have a "lag time" (the time between starting the behavior and having it become urge-driven and difficult to control) of up to seven years. Just as some people who suffer from alcoholism may have a problem almost immediately upon starting to drink, while others drink for years before developing alcoholism, the lag time for impulse control disorders also varies. Although information about what factors predict a shorter lag time is limited, early evidence suggests that starting the behavior at a later age and having a family history of psychiatric illness may predict a shorter lag time before developing symptoms of the actual disorder.

There is also some indication that impulse control disorders that begin in childhood or adolescence may differ from those with a later age of onset. For example, is kleptomania that begins at age thirteen the same as kleptomania that starts in adulthood? Is one version more likely to be of genetic origin? Due to infectious agents? Or due to a particular life event? Is an early-onset impulse control disorder easier or harder to treat? And should the treatments differ based on age of onset? Currently, our knowledge in this area is lacking, but answers to these questions may begin to address the larger issue of etiology and may improve treatment.

The impulse control behaviors often begin as relatively normal behaviors and without any defined stress. In the case of compulsive shopping or compulsive sex, the development of an actual disorder usually begins without any warning after the person has been engaging in the behaviors in an enjoyable and responsible way for a long period of time. In the case of the other disorders, people report gambling innocently with friends as entertainment for years before developing a problem. Kleptomaniacs may report several minor thefts, often beginning when they were children, without any related problems. Although kleptomania has long been thought to occur secondary to emotional loss, there is no systematic evidence that notable events give rise to uncontrollable stealing. For example, Mary Jo recalls stealing when she was in college in her early twenties. She denies having any serious emotional problems at that time. Instead, she reports that although she generally had had no monetary problems and had never wanted for things, certain items in stores, such as sweaters, preoccupied her. "It felt funny when I would enter a store. I always had plenty of money, but I remember stealing from a very young age. It was only when I began college, however, that I felt I couldn't stop the stealing."

Many professionals have thought that the onset of these behaviors is associated with some sort of loss, change in life, or pronounced emotional state. For example, perhaps people start their compulsive shopping or compulsive gambling when they are faced with a divorce or when the family is disrupted in some way. However, although many people report that they engage in various behaviors in response to social and/or emotional circumstances, there does not appear to be any association between events such as these and the development of an actual impulse control disorder. For example, a young man may start gambling almost every night after his wife leaves him. This man may gamble because he is lonely or to escape his emotional pain. This does not mean, however, that he suffers from pathological gambling disorder. As we will discuss, in an impulse control disorder, the behavior is only one part of the overall illness.

Why does one person gamble and another shop too much? What explains the exact behavioral manifestation of these urges to engage in addictive behaviors? Although people with impulse control disorders probably have a genetic vulnerability to addictive behaviors, mimicking the behavior of another person ("modeling") may explain why some people engage in certain impulse behaviors and not others. In the case of gambling, many men report that their initial exposure was when they watched their fathers bet with family or friends. Marcia recalls watching her mother take items from a store when she was a little girl. "I noticed her putting things in her purse every time we went to the department store. I was only about eight years old, but I remember the secrecy of her behavior and how she tried to hide it from me and never told anyone at home." An epidemic of shoplifting among young women in nineteenth-century Paris supports the theory of modeling. The shoplifting "illness" appeared to spread and may have been reinforced by the media attention that the women received. This behavior, however, was most likely not kleptomania. Although modeling may offer clues to why people engage in certain behaviors, and may explain why similar behaviors "run in families," it does not fully explain the development of actual psychiatric disorders.

Why people develop impulse control disorders is not clear. Some people are able to cite specific events in their lives that coincided with the beginning of their illness. Is such an event the cause? Most likely not. In fact, many people try desperately to explain their behaviors, attempting to isolate a moment or an event that gave rise to their difficulties. In general, this type of exploration is not helpful. These disorders are more likely to be caused by a complex interaction of genetics, developmental events, and environmental influences. Some of these factors, as we will explain, are just beginning to be explored.

How Long Does an Impulse Control Disorder Persist?

Because of the limited amount of research on impulse control disorders and the lack of longitudinal studies, there is no definitive answer to the question of how long an impulse control disorder persists. Our clinical experience suggests that impulse control disorders generally appear to be chronic conditions. In fact, most of the people we treat have been engaging in these behaviors for years before seeking treatment. Few of these patients have had any significant amount of time without symptoms of the disorder (usually just a few months at most). Thus, identification and early treatment will potentially improve the course of the illness.

Kathleen, a forty-six-year-old mother of three children, had been gambling for the past eighteen years. Although she initially gambled only a few times a year, this had progressed to weekly gambling for the past twelve years. Kathleen could hardly recall a period of time when she did not have urges to gamble. "I gamble every week, but I want to gamble more often—probably every day. I don't because of fear that my husband will leave me if it becomes a huge problem. I have urges to gamble all the time. I think I have gone one or two weeks in the past without the cravings, but that's it. They're always with me. Even after I gave birth to my children, when most women would only be thinking about the baby, I was thinking about how soon I would feel better and be able to gamble."

Kathleen's gambling problem is not unlike most of our patients' problems. Even when gamblers and shoppers are out of money, or when kleptomaniacs are in jail, the symptoms seem to persist. They may not engage in the behavior, but the desire to do so remains.

William, who suffered from kleptomania, moved to a farm in another state to get away from stores. "I thought that if there was no temptation, I wouldn't or couldn't steal. I even asked my wife to always go to town for me to keep me out of stores. It didn't seem to make a difference. I went a year without stealing, but I wanted to steal all the time. I was still tormented by my thoughts and desires."

With the proper medication and therapy, significant improvements in the urges and the behavior associated with particular impulse control disorders have been reported. Several studies provide hope regarding the treatment of these disorders. People with impulse control disorders should know that they may benefit significantly from appropriate treatment.

Questions to Ask

How do you know if you or someone you know is suffering from an impulse control disorder? There are no blood tests, brain-scanning techniques, or other "scientific" means of diagnosing these illnesses. Instead, psychiatric diagnoses are made primarily on the basis of asking questions to see whether the DSM-IV criteria for a disorder are fulfilled. In the case of compulsive shopping or compulsive sexual behavior—disorders that lack DSM-IV criteria—generally agreed upon criteria must be satisfied.

The following sets of questions are useful in making the diagnoses of various impulse control disorders. The questions mirror the DSM-IV criteria or reflect the generally agreed upon conceptualizations of the disorders. In the case of compulsive shopping, the questions presented owe a deep debt to the work of Dr. Susan McElroy at the University of Cincinnati for her initial conceptualization of this disorder and to Dr. Donald Black at the University of Iowa for his early pioneering work on compulsive shopping. The questions for compulsive sexual behavior owe much to the groundbreaking research of Eli Coleman, Ph.D., at the University of Minnesota.

Pathological Gambling Questionnaire

1. Do thoughts of gambling preoccupy you? That is, do you think about gambling a lot and wish you could think about it less?

   Yes   No

2. Have you been unable to stop gambling or decrease the amount you gamble?

   Yes   No

3. When you tried to stop or cut down, did you feel more irritable or anxious?

   Yes   No

4. Has the amount you need to gamble to get the same sort of "high" or excitement increased?

   Yes   No

5. Do you gamble as a way of escaping feelings of depression?

   Yes   No

6. After you lose, do you go back in the next couple of days to try to win back the money?

   Yes   No

7. What effect has your gambling had on your life? Have you:
   - Lied to others about your gambling?   Yes   No
   - Committed illegal acts?   Yes   No
   - Found that it significantly interfered with school, job, or relationships?   Yes   No
   - Needed to borrow money?   Yes   No

8. When you aren't gambling, do you have urges to gamble?

   Yes   No

A person is likely to be suffering from pathological gambling disorder if he or she answered yes to five or more of the questions. The last question is not part of the DSM criteria but is a useful question when one is trying to determine if someone has a gambling problem. Some people gamble in binges—for example, they may gamble only when they have available funds. However, these people may be significantly impaired by the cravings or urges to gamble even though they may not have actually gambled for weeks.

Kleptomania Questionnaire

1. Do you steal or have urges to steal things?

   Yes   No

2. Do thoughts of stealing or urges to steal preoccupy you? That is, do you think about stealing or have urges to steal a lot and wish the thoughts or urges were less?

   Yes   No

3. Do you feel tense or anxious before you steal or when you have urges to steal?

   Yes   No

4. Has the stealing or the urges to steal caused you a lot of distress?

   Yes   No

5. Has the stealing or the urges to steal significantly interfered with your life in some way?

   Yes   No

You may be suffering from kleptomania if you answered yes to questions 1 and 2 and yes to questions 3, 4, or 5. This questionnaire differs from the DSM criteria in that it does not ask whether the items stolen are needed or for personal use. While many people with kleptomania report stealing peculiar items, many also report that it is the urge to steal that is out of control. Therefore, many patients tell me that if they have severe urges to take things, they feel that they might as well risk getting caught for something they can use or want. In these cases, it may appear that the person is simply a thief or antisocial. The difference between thieves and people with kleptomania, however, is that thieves can control their behavior and can choose not to steal, whereas people with kleptomania have little control over their behavior because of the urges to steal.

Compulsive Shopping Questionnaire

1. Do you shop frequently, buying more than you can afford, buying items that you do not need, or buying for longer periods of time than you intended?

   Yes   No

2. Do you have urges to buy things?

   Yes   No

3. Do thoughts of shopping or urges to shop preoccupy you? That is, do you think about shopping or have urges to shop a lot and wish the thoughts or urges were less?

   Yes   No

4. Has the shopping or the urges to shop caused you a lot of distress?

   Yes   No

5. Has the shopping or the urges to shop significantly interfered with your life in some way?

   Yes   No

You may be suffering from compulsive shopping if you answered yes to question 1, either question 2 or question 3, and either question 4 or question 5. While excessive shopping behavior is usually present in compulsive shoppers, the behavior alone appears insufficient to warrant a psychiatric diagnosis. Instead, most compulsive shoppers are preoccupied by either thoughts about shopping or urges to shop, and this criterion is essential to the diagnosis.

Compulsive Sexual Behavior Questionnaire

1. Do you have excessive or uncontrolled sexual behavior or sexual urges?

                                                    Yes   No

2. Do you have excessive or uncontrolled sexual thoughts?

                                                    Yes   No

3. Has the sexual behavior, thoughts, or urges caused you a lot of distress?

                                                    Yes   No

4. Has the sex or the urges to have sex significantly interfered with your life in some way?

                                                    Yes   No

If you answered yes to either question 1 or question 2 and another yes to either question 3 or question 4, then you may have a problem with compulsive sexual behavior.

One note of caution about all of these questionnaires: They are intended as screening instruments, not diagnostic instruments. What this means is that the questionnaires may suggest that a disorder is present, but they cannot make the actual diagnosis of an illness. Instead, a face-to-face interview with a trained clinician is needed to determine the diagnosis. Therefore, clinical judgment should always be used to confirm answers to a self-report questionnaire.

4

The Impact of Impulse Control Disorders

"I Could've Done So Much More with My Life": Impact on School and Work

"I used to have a good job, but I just couldn't do it anymore," Patrick began. He had come to see me after having lost his wife and his house as a result of gambling debt. Patrick was severely depressed, thinking about suicide as the only solution to his problems. "I can't believe that my life has taken the course it has—primarily because of my gambling addiction."

Patrick had grown up in a family that didn't gamble. He had always been a good student in high school; he was popular and never got into any trouble. After high school, Patrick attended a private college with the intention of becoming an engineer. He started encountering difficulties toward the end of college. Having started to gamble casually with friends, Patrick gradually became more involved in various types of wagering. He would spend hours playing cards with anyone he could find. Other times, he would go to the horse track. Patrick's parents trusted their son and didn't appear to notice when he asked for increasingly larger sums of money "for school." "I felt guilty lying to my parents. I would call them and say I needed more money for books or something. The lies grew bigger as my debt increased. I was losing several hundred dollars each month. It was tearing me up inside, but I couldn't stop. If you told me I was throwing away my parents' last dollars, I don't think even that would have stopped me."

Patrick started to miss classes, and his grades suffered. "I saw my grades slipping, and I was scared, but for some reason I couldn't stop myself. Why didn't I go for help sooner? Although school was never hard for me, I saw the effects of my addiction. I used to be a great student. After I started gambling, I was doing O.K., but I could've done so much better. When I graduated, I had to take a second-rate job because my grades had fallen so much. I was so disappointed in myself. I didn't know then that it was only the first of many dreams gambling would ruin."

Patrick worked as an engineer, but only for a short time. "The disappointments just kept coming. I just couldn't work when I preferred to gamble. All day I thought about gambling. It was all I wanted to do. Work became a nuisance—it was something that got in the way of gambling. So I quit." Patrick left his engineering job and took a job as a waiter. "The waiter job gives me more control over my hours. If I want to stay at the casino all night and the racetrack all day, I can. I just trade shifts.

"I have thrown away an education and am working at a job I hate, all because of gambling. It's ruined my life. This isn't who I wanted to be, but I don't feel like I have control over that any longer." Patrick's depression became so severe that he attempted suicide.

Krystal, a fifteen-year-old, was brought to the clinic by her parents. "At first her grades dropped. Now she won't go to school because of this problem." Krystal's parents were referring to their daughter's stealing. "She used to steal just from people in the family. Over the last year, she has been stealing from stores and from other children at school. At the same time, she lost interest in school. Her grades suffered. She was such a good student, interested in school. Now we can't even force her to go. If she does go to school, she often misses classes."

Krystal had sat silent throughout the initial interview. When asked what she thought was going on, she started crying, "I don't want to see the other kids—I've stolen from so many of them. I wish I could stop doing it, but I can't. I want to go to school. I really like school, but I'm so embarrassed. I need to get good grades. I want to go to college and be a nurse. But I just can't concentrate. Every time I try to study, I just think about stealing things. I can't control the urges to steal. I keep telling myself I have to study, but it's no use."

Krystal had started stealing about two years prior to my seeing her. Although she had initially stolen only occasionally, the frequency of her stealing had gradually increased. "I used to have days when I didn't do it, and I thought maybe it was over, that I would never do it again. But I was wrong. Now, it's all I do and all I think about." When she was at school, Krystal started to steal from the other students and from the school, taking items such as bracelets and books. "The other kids think I'm some sort of criminal."

"I could've done so much more with my life, but my shopping ruined everything," Jill told me as she took a seat in my office. "I've been at that company for fifteen years, and I have been an exceptional employee. If I didn't have this shopping problem, I would have gotten that promotion." Jill, a corporate executive in her thirties, had earned an M.B.A. degree and had a job at a prestigious corporation. Over the years, she had become known in the company as a person who placed work above all else, often staying late during the week and working many weekends and holidays. When she was not working, Jill had always enjoyed shopping, but she had never spent extravagantly and had always paid her credit card bills in full.

"Maybe it was the increased pressure I felt at work, but around six months ago, I began shopping on my lunch breaks. It started as a way to relax, to get away from the stress at work. It became an almost daily activity, but it didn't get in the way of work at first. About three months ago, I noticed a change. When I got to work, I started to think or fantasize about the things I would buy at lunch. It became difficult to concentrate on work. I even starting bringing catalogues to the office and reading them instead of doing my work. I kept telling myself that tomorrow I would get serious about work, but it never happened."

Jill started increasing the amount of time she took for her lunch breaks, often staying away from the office for two or three hours. Eventually she stopped coming back to the office after lunch. "I would start shopping, and before I knew it, the afternoon was gone. I hated myself. I knew I had a problem, and yet I felt incapable of correcting it." Jill's work suffered, and when the senior partners in the corporation made promotion decisions, Jill's name was not on the list. "I felt so cheated, and I hated myself. I didn't know this was an illness. I just thought I was self-destructive or something."

The urges and behaviors associated with impulse control disorders make it difficult for people to concentrate on work or school. As a result, many people take longer to complete projects or simply fail to finish required tasks. Of the people we've treated, approximately 60 to 70 percent report that their school or work performance has been negatively affected by their illnesses. But this isn't only because of poor concentration. Many people report that the urges to engage in impulsive behavior are so intense that they cannot stay in school or at work. In fact, they may not even go to work or to school, choosing instead to gamble, shop, or steal.

The desire to engage in impulsive behaviors often leads people to accept employment positions that are more suited to their addictive behavior. Patrick took a job as a waiter to accommodate his gambling. Sharon, also a pathological gambler, left her job as a respiratory therapist to drive a taxi. "I could make my own hours. Staying at the casino for a day or two wouldn't get in the way of this job. I could just work more hours later in the week." The decision to change one's career in order to accommodate uncontrollable behavior, however, often leads to feelings of powerlessness, depression, and hopelessness. "When I gave up the job I loved and took another job just because I wanted to gamble, that's when I knew this illness was controlling me. It's also when I gave up hope of beating this problem." Melissa left her job as a receptionist. "I couldn't sit there all day. I needed to be out, in case I could find a guy for sex. Restraining my urges for sex was so uncomfortable. I took a job in deliveries instead. Now I get out, look for guys, and still do my work." Of the patients we have treated, approximately 20 to 25 percent are currently working in positions that they feel are beneath their potential. And they attribute their choice of employment to their illnesses.

Even caring for family members may suffer. Charles, a father of two small children, worked at home on data processing. As his compulsive shopping worsened, he found it more difficult to care for his children. Charles's wife noticed firsthand the disabling effects of the illness. "I came home one day to find that he had failed to feed our children. They were crying and he didn't seem to notice. Instead, he was buying something on the Internet." Charles's wife left him and took the two children.

But like the disorders themselves, problems with work and school can range from mild to severe. Many people function quite well despite their illness. Others find that their grades or job performance drop. On average, the longer an impulse disorder goes untreated, the greater the likelihood that school or work will suffer. Also, as people have more problems at school or work, they may find escape in their behaviors, and so a vicious cycle can be created. When impulse control disorders respond to psychiatric treatment, however, school and work functioning usually improves, sometimes quickly and quite dramatically.

"I Feel Ashamed When I Look at My Children's Faces": Impact on Social and Personal Relationships

Avoidance is one common aspect of impulse control disorders. It may take many forms, and it may damage relationships in many ways. For instance, many people with impulse control disorders avoid family or friends out of shame and embarrassment. Ian, a forty-two-year-old with compulsive sexual behavior, avoided his friends and became more socially isolated as his illness progressed. "Every time I saw them, I was reminded of how my life was so disgusting. My friends are good people, with morals. Being with them made me feel bad about myself. It was easier just to cut ties." Stephanie, a mother of two adolescent children, gradually began to do less with her children as her kleptomania went untreated. "I felt so dirty because of what I was doing. How can I tell my children to be moral and do the right thing when I'm stealing? I feel ashamed every time I look into my children's faces. I just pulled away. It broke my heart to do so. I traded one pain for another."

Over 90 percent of the people we've interviewed who have an impulse control disorder report feelings of shame or embarrassment concerning their behavior—in the cases of kleptomania and compulsive sexual behavior, it's 100 percent. Many people with these illnesses withdraw from the world at least to some extent. Depression is common. Family members are often confused and hurt by the patient's avoidance of family or social events. The patient may appear anxious, self-conscious, and preoccupied. Family members recognize that there has been a change but do not know how to intervene because often they do not know what the problem really is.

Impulse control disorders may also cause significant interference with intimate relationships. In these cases, avoidance often takes the form of failing to talk about the illness with one's significant other. Most of the people with impulse control disorders that we treat (70 to 80 percent) are either married or in long-term relationships. Approximately two-thirds of the gamblers and compulsive shoppers we treat, however, have not discussed their illness with their significant other. In the case of kleptomania and compulsive sexual behavior, the percentage is closer to 97 percent. It is not uncommon for patients to tell us that we are the first person they have talked to about their problem, even if the problem has been ongoing for several years.

"I've been gambling weekly for almost fifteen years, and I haven't told my husband," Megan began. "He thinks I go visit my sister on Friday nights. I can stay out all night, and he has no clue what I'm up to. It hurts me to lie to him, but I think it would bother me more if he knew. The problem is that gambling has become a big part of my life, and he knows nothing about it. How can I have a good marriage when I leave him out of such a large part of my life?"

Sharon, a fifty-six-year-old married woman, had been shopping compulsively for twelve years without telling her husband. "I sold my wedding ring," Sharon said as she began to cry. "I had to sell it to pay my credit card bills. I work so hard to keep this problem from my husband. The lying has torn my marriage apart. I've become distant. I'm so scared that if I get close to him, I might let the shopping problem slip out. I'm too embarrassed about it even to tell the man I've lived with for thirty years. I know I'm hurting him by being so cold, but I'd rather do that than tell him I have this problem. What kind of wife am I?"

Some people with impulse control disorders avoid various types of social interactions because of the urges and preoccupations associated with these disorders. Garret, a forty-two-year-old father of three children, began to miss his children's school activities because of his gambling urges. "I became so overwhelmed by the urge to gamble and the thought of gambling that I would miss my children's events at school because I couldn't resist going to the casino and gambling. I wanted to be with my children, and I had every intention of going to these events. But I just couldn't. I feel I'm a horrible father." Sandy started missing social events with her friends because the urges to steal were so intense. "I would start getting ready to go out, and then I would get this urge to steal. I often couldn't stop myself. I found myself calling my friends on numerous occasions and telling them I wasn't feeling well. Instead, I would go to stores and steal something. After a while, they quit calling. I think I've lost a few good friends because of my stealing."

People with impulse control disorders may also avoid certain situations or places as a means of preventing their behavior. Kathy, a married woman with two children, felt that the only way she could stop her stealing was by not going to stores. "I just resolved that I wouldn't go to stores. This obviously caused a lot of tension with my husband. For years I had been doing the grocery shopping and buying clothes for the children. I just stopped. The problem was that I couldn't tell my husband why. Instead, I told him he had to do these jobs. Because he worked outside of the home and I didn't, he started to resent me for this. We had many quarrels about this decision of mine. After almost losing my marriage, however, I went back to the stores and back to stealing."

Eric, a young man with compulsive sexual behavior, decided not to leave his home for any reason. He didn't go to work or even run simple errands. "I enjoy the sex, but I hate myself for having to do it. So I decided that if I didn't leave my house, I couldn't engage in this behavior. I bought weeks' worth of canned food and just hid away. The problem was that even though I wasn't having sex, I was still thinking about it and wanting to have sex. I was no longer tortured by my behavior, but I was still bothered by my thoughts and desires."

In most cases of impulse control disorders, avoiding the behavior does not result in decreased urges or thoughts. In fact, the majority of people report that avoidance of the behavior, at least in the short term, actually intensifies the urges and thoughts. Bonnie described her sexual feelings: "I could go for days without sex, but it was just delaying the inevitable. The urges to have sex never went away; instead, they seemed to get worse with time." Approximately one-quarter of the people we've interviewed have become housebound for at least a week to avoid their behaviors. Most of these people engaged in the impulsive behavior to an even greater extent after they discontinued the forced imprisonment. Although refraining from various behaviors for an extended period of time may in fact decrease the urges and thoughts, to do so would result in severe dysfunction for most people. A person should not have to become housebound indefinitely to correct impulsive behavior; in fact, this type of deprivation does more harm than good, as it reinforces the social stigma of these disorders. As we discuss later, there appear to be promising treatment options for these disorders, so that people do not have to avoid living.

Should People with Impulse Control Disorders Tell Family and Friends?

People with impulse control disorders often ask us whether they should tell their family or friends about their behavior. This is usually a very complicated question with no simple answer. People with impulse control disorders may ask this because they are ashamed of their behavior and want some type of forgiveness from loved ones. They may be tired of the secrecy and the worries about getting caught. They may feel that they love their family and that withholding this personal information is dishonest. Finally, some people realize that they have an illness and want help and support in learning to cope with this difficulty.

Gail, a fifty-four-year-old woman who suffered from kleptomania, wanted her family to come to an appointment. "I just think it's time I tell them. I can't keep living like this. They know nothing about the things I've done. They think I've been a great mother and wife. They aren't aware of the awful things I've done."

"Why do you think they should know?" I asked her.

"I feel so guilty and dirty about all of the items I've stolen. They love their image of me. I want them to see the real me. I hope they can forgive me for all the lies."

After much consultation, Gail insisted on bringing her family to an appointment. With much crying, the family was able to discuss Gail's kleptomania and support her in her treatment. Not everyone, however, is as lucky as Gail.

One woman we were treating for pathological gambling decided that her husband should know how they had really lost their savings. Previously she had lied to him, giving serious health concerns and exorbitant medical bills as the reason their savings were depleted. She decided to tell her husband the truth because she felt it was dishonest not to let him know and because the guilt of not having told him for years was troubling her enormously. However, when she told him that she was a gambler and had lost the money through multiple casino visits, her husband was not supportive. At the appointment where she told him of the gambling problem, he said to her, "I don't care so much about the money. The fact that you've had this problem for three years and didn't tell me about it says we have problems much larger than money." After several failed attempts at marital counseling, her husband left her.

Lawrence, a compulsive shopper who had serious financial difficulties and depression, wanted to tell his wife about his disorder. However, he was worried that she would not understand. "I want my wife to know because I shouldn't have to go through this all by myself. She married me for better or for worse. I can't imagine it getting worse than this. I lost my job. We have no health insurance. We have $80,000 in credit card bills. I need help, but I also need someone to love me during this ordeal. I know I have a disease, but it sounds so trivial to talk about having a shopping problem. I have the problem, and I'm not sure even I can take it seriously. How do I explain this illness to other people?"

"I feel like I have some secret life that my friends don't know about," Frank explained about his compulsive sexual behavior. "We make plans to go places, but I'd rather be looking for sex. I spend so much of my time cruising around trying to find men to have sex with that I don't do anything with my friends any longer. I seem to need to do it for my ego. I mean, I feel attractive or wanted when I find someone. Otherwise I guess I don't like myself too much."

"Do you feel guilty about your behavior?" I asked.

"I wouldn't say guilty," Frank responded. "I just don't feel comfortable telling my friends. I have a constant need for sex, and it's destroying my friendships. Should I tell them?"

There is no single correct answer to any of these questions. It is often useful to compare the pros and cons of telling personal information to others. Because impulse control disorders present in different ways for different people, and because the ways in which these disorders disrupt lives and families may differ, this advice may not benefit everyone with an impulse control disorder. Having said that, when people wish to tell family and friends, we often advise them to take a few days before making a final decision about whom to tell and what to tell. People with impulse control disorders suffer from serious psychiatric illnesses. They are entitled to receive support and care from their loved ones. When told of these problems, however, family and friends may not respond to the information with the response the person expects or hopes for.

For instance, one woman told her family about her compulsive shopping problem. The family was very supportive of her and helped her through treatment. After treatment, however, with her symptoms in remission, the woman told me, "My family treats me like I'm a child. They watch my money. I can't go out alone. They always ask me where I'm going, even if I just want to take a walk. I feel like I've been branded."

Although these illnesses may be frustrating and even frightening for family and friends, people with impulse control disorders deserve the support of their loved ones. However, a common source of problems between people with impulse control disorders and their loved ones is the lack of information that most family members have regarding these disorders. They are often unsure how to respond to the news of the illness and unsure as to what their role should be. The people we treat often invite members of their family or their close friends to come to appointments. The purpose of these meetings is to clarify what the illness means, what causes it, how we're going to treat it, and, most importantly, what the loved ones can do for the person who is suffering from one of these disorders.

Depression, Hospitalization, and Suicide

Approximately one-third of the people we interview tell us that they have battled with depression at some point in their lives. It is often difficult to determine whether the depression resulted from the impulsive behavior or contributed to the behavior. Many people tell us that they did not have problems with their mood before the impulsive behavior started. "I don't remember feeling depressed until I started gambling," Paul began. "Now I feel so hopeless, especially when I return home from the casino. It's not just when I lose, although it's worse then. Even when I win, I often feel depressed."

Others, however, report that the impulsive behavior may actually help alleviate their depression. "Sex soothes me," Michelle explained. "When I get upset about things at work or with my boyfriend, having sex with some stranger makes me feel better." Karni, a thirty-seven-year-old who suffered from kleptomania, described how stealing things often made her mood better, if only for a few minutes. "The act of stealing gives me a slight euphoric feeling. When I'm depressed, it can help my mood. The problem is that the relief only lasts for a few minutes, and then I feel even worse." Andrew, a compulsive shopper, provided a similar viewpoint: "I think the only time I'm not depressed is when I'm shopping. Then I get home, and I realize that I didn't need or want the things I bought. The bills keep piling up, and I have worse financial worries. The happiness from shopping is just an illusion, but at the time I'm doing it, I love it."

The relationship between a person's mood and impulsive behavior is quite complicated, and often a vicious cycle is created.

Many people with impulse control disorders have isolated themselves from family and friends because of their behavior. Timothy, a pathological gambler, had avoided family functions for two years, choosing instead to go to the local casinos whenever he had free time. Avoiding social activities led to feelings of social isolation, loneliness, and depression. Timothy's only feeling of social connection came from going to the casino, and so when he felt lonely, Timothy would return to the casino. The casino had effectively replaced his family.

Whether the depression or the impulse control disorder comes first is not always clear. What is clear, however, is that they seem to feed each other. Depression worsens the impulsive behavior, and the impulsive behavior worsens the feelings of depression.

When people engage in impulsive behavior to escape from boredom or depression, depression is the primary problem. The depression may be relieved by the behavior (even if only for a short period), but at the expense of the impulsive behavior. On the other hand, in the case of primary impulsive behavior, impulsive symptoms may be relieved by the behavior (even though it may be a short-lasting relief), but at the expense of depression.

Hospitalization as a result of an impulse control disorder is relatively common. About one-quarter of the people we treat have been hospitalized at some point in their lives. The reasons for hospitalization vary. Of those who have been hospitalized, less than 20 percent have told their physician or their family about their impulse control disorder, even though 95 percent reported that the impulse control disorder was the primary reason for their hospitalization.

Rochelle, a seventy-four-year-old woman suffering from compulsive shopping, was hospitalized after trying to kill herself. "I realized a few years ago I had a problem with buying things. It didn't cause real financial trouble, so I never thought about getting help. The month before I went to the hospital, however, I was having serious difficulties paying the credit card bills. I had to ask my oldest son for money. I couldn't tell him why I needed it, and so I made up a lie about some failed investments. I felt like a failure, both as a person and as a mother. I had no self-esteem. I was so worried about the bills that I couldn't sleep. I spent the days crying. I couldn't stop thinking about the bills and how many silly things I had purchased. I felt like I was falling apart. That's when I took the pills." Rochelle spent two weeks in the hospital. She never mentioned her shopping problem to her family or to the psychiatrist treating her. "It just sounds like such a silly problem. I'm afraid no one would take me seriously."

Suicidal thinking is common among people who suffer from impulse control disorders. Approximately 50 to 60 percent of the patients we see have had thoughts of suicide that they have attributed primarily or entirely to their impulse control disorder. Attempts at suicide are also not uncommon. About 10 to 15 percent of my patients have made a suicide attempt. These numbers reflect the shame, embarrassment, and personal torment that people with impulse control disorders feel. The rate of completed suicide among people with impulse control disorders is not known, but some people with impulse control disorders do kill themselves.

Monica, a fifty-three-year-old married housewife, suffered from kleptomania for about twenty years. I never met Monica, but her husband related her story to me after he read about my treatment for kleptomania. "My wife was tormented for twenty years. I never knew how much she suffered. I only found out after she killed herself and I found her diary. She had been stealing almost daily. She never wanted to steal things. She couldn't stop herself. She was a good person. She was also a good mother and wife. She went to church and volunteered in community organizations. She was confused about this other side of herself. She was so ashamed she could never tell me about it. Instead, she lived all alone with the pain and embarrassment. I wish she had let me know what she was going through. One weekend when I was out of town on business, Monica overdosed on sleeping pills. I can only imagine how alone she felt. I wish she had asked for help." We have no doubt that psychiatric treatment of impulse control disorders may prevent many such cases of suicide.

"Alcohol Is My Only Way to Cope": Alcohol and Drug Abuse

One common way of coping with impulse control disorders is to drink or use drugs. With respect to alcohol and drug use, impulse control disorders are not all alike. In the cases of compulsive shopping and compulsive sexual behavior that we see, drug or alcohol use is rare. Approximately one-fifth of the people with kleptomania that we see, however, have a current or past problem with alcohol or drugs. In the cases of pathological gambling that we treat, probably one-fourth to one-third have a current or past problem with drugs or alcohol. In all of these cases, the intent behind the drug or alcohol use is generally similar—to escape the thoughts, urges, and problems associated with the behavior.

Theresa, a forty-one-year-old office manager, described how she used alcohol to cope with her gambling addiction. "I drink almost every day after I'm done gambling. I never drink while I'm gambling because it dulls my thinking. After I leave the casino and get home, however, I drink myself to sleep. I never had a problem with drinking until I started to gamble." Theresa had been fired because of her alcohol use, and after she had an accident, the court ordered her to undergo treatment. "I needed treatment for gambling, not alcohol. It was like putting a small bandage on a huge wound." Within four days of discharge from treatment, Theresa was back at the casino. Within two weeks of leaving treatment, she had started drinking again.

Stephen, a twenty-eight-year-old who suffered from kleptomania, also struggled with cocaine addiction. "I use cocaine because it stops me from stealing. When I use it, I don't have the urges to steal. I can get away from those urges and thoughts for a while. I know it sounds crazy: I escape one illegal behavior by doing another. But the stealing urges are so overpowering, I can't resist them otherwise. I'd rather use cocaine at home than go to jail. Also, I don't feel guilty about using cocaine. Stealing breaks one of the Commandments. Drug use doesn't."

It is not always clear whether the impulse control disorder causes the alcohol or drug problem. Edith, a forty-year-old pathological gambler, described her drinking problem this way: "I think I've had a problem with alcohol since my early twenties. When I started to gamble, years later, however, the alcohol problem seemed to get a lot worse. I can't say gambling made me an alcoholic, but I know gambling made it more likely. Now, alcohol is my only way to cope." Determining which problem came first, or how they interact, can be difficult. Often both the impulse control disorder and the drug or alcohol problem need to be treated simultaneously. Many patients that we treat, however, believe that their alcohol or drug problem arose largely because of the behavior associated with their impulse control disorder. Given that alcohol is often served in casinos, this may in fact be the case for many pathological gamblers. Because these people are often too embarrassed to discuss their impulse behavior, we routinely ask all people with alcohol or drug problems whether they have symptoms of an impulse control disorder.

"I Never Thought I Was Capable of These Things": Criminal Activity and Other Legal Consequences

Emily, a forty-seven-year-old mother of four children, came to my office in tears for her first visit. "I never thought I was capable of these things. I have always tried to live a moral life. I've never had legal problems, and now this." Emily sobbed so hard she couldn't speak for several minutes. When she had composed herself, she told her story. "I have a gambling problem. It's been out of control for about two years. I gamble several times every week and lose hundreds of dollars. We aren't rich. My husband works so hard, and I'm just adding to the problem. I've cleaned out our savings. I've stolen from my husband's wallet when he's asleep. I even stole from my ten-year-old son's piggy bank. But I didn't stop there. This is so hard to talk about, and I'm so ashamed." Emily again broke into tears. "I started forging checks. Neighbors, friends, family—it didn't matter whose checks. I probably forged $10,000 worth of checks over the last four months. I have no friends left. My family wants nothing to do with me. And I think my husband's going to leave me. I deserve it."

Andrew, a bank executive, told a similar story. "My compulsive shopping got so out of control. My credit card debt was huge. I couldn't pay it back. And even with all the debt, I still wanted to buy things. Financial fears would bother me every night—I couldn't sleep. I would lie in bed drenched in sweat. And yet, in the morning I would make lists of the things I 'needed' to buy."

"What legal problems did your compulsive shopping cause you?" I asked.

"I stole from my clients. I basically embezzled money. I was raised with values. As I was stealing the money, I knew it was wrong. But I was so desperate. I got caught recently. It's terrifying to think about what I have become—a criminal."

Legal problems as a result of impulse control disorders are relatively common. Except for perhaps alcohol and drug use, no other illnesses are so closely linked with illegal behavior. Kleptomania, or compulsive shoplifting, by definition involves illegal behavior. Pathological gambling may involve illegal forms of gambling, but most commonly the person engages in illegal behavior in order to pay the debts that result from gambling. Compulsive shopping, like gambling, is associated with illegal behavior secondary to the debt that most compulsive shoppers acquire. And compulsive sexual behavior often involves illegal behavior (public sexual conduct, prostitution, etc.).

Among the pathological gamblers that we treat, approximately one-fourth have had legal difficulties. An additional one-fourth have filed for bankruptcy. For most gamblers, their dealings with the legal system are limited to filing for bankruptcy. For many people, however, bankruptcy can be a devastating experience. For Ruth, a fifty-three-year-old bank executive, filing for bankruptcy added to the already significant shame that she felt concerning her gambling. "I knew I had a problem, but when I filed for bankruptcy, the enormity of my problem suddenly hit me. I had lost everything. I was embarrassed by my problem, but I never let anyone know. Now the newspapers mentioned my bankruptcy. It was like I announced to the whole community that I was out of control." Ruth eventually sold her house and moved to another state. "I couldn't hold my head up anymore. It was either move or kill myself."

Other people that we treat erroneously think of bankruptcy as an easy answer to their debt. They believe it will free them from their credit card debt without any repercussions. Timothy, a twenty-nine-year-old consultant, had significant credit card debt as a result of gambling. "I think I acquired about forty thousand dollars of debt within a few months. It was scary. I couldn't make the monthly interest payments. Then someone told me to file for bankruptcy—that it would solve my problems. I was so desperate I'd have done anything." Timothy responded well to medication and therapy and has not gambled for about a year. He regrets, however, having filed for bankruptcy. "It's caused problems for me. I can't get new credit cards. I wanted to buy a house, but the bankruptcy has ruined my credit history. I wish I had thought about it more carefully."

Although many people may in fact need to file for bankruptcy, the decision to do so must be thought about carefully. It is not just an easy way to avoid paying one's debts. Federal bankruptcy laws are constantly changing, and many of the changes that have been made recently have had the effect of making both the filing requirements and the repercussions more serious. Anyone who is considering filing for bankruptcy should talk to an attorney who specializes in that field to learn about both the short-term and long-term ramifications of the decision.

But the legal problems of pathological gamblers often extend beyond just filing for bankruptcy. In fact, about one-fourth of our patients have resorted to various illegal activities to cope with their gambling debts. Many people may knowingly write bad checks to cover other expenses, such as credit card payments, groceries, or the heating bill. Many people become quite desperate when faced with increasing debt; they may embezzle money from their employer, knowingly commit tax fraud, or even steal from strangers. Sheila, a divorced mother of three children, had a severe gambling problem, with her debt exceeding her income as a cashier. "I started to prostitute myself for extra money. You cannot imagine the shame and disgust I feel about myself. I was at the end of my rope. The gambling just got worse. I had to feed my kids."

In the case of kleptomania, the defining behavior is itself illegal, and this is why many people with this problem do not seek treatment. One man told us, "When I set up this appointment, I was sure that the police would be waiting for me. I thought about canceling several times because of the fear that the police would be here." A woman described her fear of even talking with our clinic on the phone. "I feel so guilty that I don't even think rationally at times. When I first spoke with you on the phone, I was sure that the police were either listening in or tracing the call. I wanted to speak for only a few minutes because I thought that way it couldn't be traced. Who can live with this constant fear and guilt? It almost prevented me from seeking help."

"I commit a crime several days every week," Kevin began as he took a seat in my office. "How can I feel anything but disgust with myself when I keep doing this sort of thing?" I asked Kevin about any legal problems resulting from his kleptomania. "I've never been caught. I guess I just don't look like a criminal. Sometimes I wish I would get arrested. Maybe then I'd quit doing it." While one might think being apprehended would reduce the urge to steal, it does so for only a few days. After that time, people report that the urges return to their usual frequency and intensity.

Unlike Kevin, most of the people we treat for kleptomania have been apprehended at some point in their lives. These people have been stealing numerous times every week for, on average, ten to twenty years by the time they see us for treatment. Even with these patterns of behavior, however, most people have been apprehended at most once or twice in their lives. The deterrent effect of worrying about being apprehended by police may therefore be quite low for many of these people. But even if these people were apprehended more frequently, there is no reason to believe that their stealing would decrease substantially. Patients tell us that when they see a police officer, they may not act on their urges to steal, but the urges do not go away. Unless they are treated, people with kleptomania could be apprehended every day without the real underlying problem being addressed.

This is not to say that being apprehended does not affect people with kleptomania. In fact, the experience of being picked up by the police or store security can worsen the severe embarrassment and shame these people suffer. Stephanie, a forty-year-old wife and mother, had been stealing for sixteen years before being arrested in a department store for stealing men's belts. Stephanie had been stealing men's clothing for years and hoarding it in the basement of her home. She had never told her husband about her illness. Describing herself as quite religious, Stephanie suffered guilt because of her behavior and had been treated for depression for many years. After her arrest, and while waiting for her husband to pick her up from the jail, Stephanie tried to kill herself by overdosing on her antidepressant with some Tylenol. "I thought I'd rather be dead than suffer the humiliation of an arrest. It's been hard enough for me to deal with this illness without having my husband and the entire community know what sort of person I am."

If people with kleptomania are so careful about stealing in the presence of police, is this really an impulsive disorder? There is a feeling among many people, even many psychiatrists, that if someone can control his or her behavior under some circumstances—for instance, when police are in a store—then that behavior is not impulsive. Prior to 1980, many psychiatrists believed that kleptomania was simply criminal behavior, not mental illness. However, unlike people who shoplift for money or who shoplift particular items, people with kleptomania are overwhelmed by urges to steal. They may in fact be able to control their urges at particular moments, such as when police are present, but the urges do not go away.

If these behaviors cannot be controlled, should people with impulse control disorders be penalized legally for them? Some people are concerned that if these illegal behaviors are considered an "illness" or the result of an illness, then defendants in legal proceedings will simply claim that they have kleptomania or pathological gambling and avoid paying the penalty for their actions. On a clinical note, none of the people we treat have asked us to justify their actions when they have had legal difficulties. In fact, most of them see the admission that they have a mental illness to be adding further insult to the injury of arrest.

The question of "excusing" behavior because of mental illness has not been explicitly addressed in the case of impulse control disorders. One area of the law that may be seen as addressing these issues is the insanity defense in criminal law. Historically, every person is presumed to be sane and to be responsible for his or her actions until proven otherwise. Many states recognize that an accused person can establish criminal insanity under the "irresistible impulse doctrine." This defense is available when a person's mind has become so impaired by a disease that the person is deprived of the mental power to control or restrain his or her actions. This standard has been used in cases of severely mentally ill people, such as schizophrenics. It has never been applied to cases of pathological gambling or kleptomania. It is also not clear whether such a standard would apply in such cases. If a person with kleptomania does not steal when she sees a police officer, then she is able to control her actions to some extent and would not benefit from this defense. If a person with pathological gambling plans to go to the casino all day and then actually goes after work, he has planned his actions and probably could not use this defense. It is possible, however, that certain people with kleptomania could make a case for the sudden or unpremeditated quality of their actions.

Do we want to punish people for behavior that they cannot control? Do we know to what extent people with impulse control disorders in fact can or cannot control their behavior? Can we punish people for their illegal actions and yet retain the notion that these are mental illnesses with urges that are often uncontrollable? How do we identify people who are simply criminals but who claim to suffer from an impulse control disorder? Impulse control disorders raise these difficult issues, which are far from being settled either legally or ethically. "I knew I had to go to jail," Alan told me after serving ninety days for stealing from a grocery store. "But I also know I suffer from kleptomania. Is it fair that I have to keep going to jail because no one has come up with a cure for my problem?"

The Social Costs of Impulse Control Disorders

In addition to the individual problems that impulse control disorders cause, there are enormous social costs associated with these disorders. In the case of pathological gambling, there have been many reports concerning the possible costs and benefits of legalized gambling in various states. The difficulty with many of these reports, however, is that they do not look specifically at pathological gambling and that there are no generally agreed upon strategies for measuring the costs to society. Having said that, we can still see that a disorder such as pathological gambling may have significant social costs attached to it. For example, the legal difficulties of people with pathological gambling have social, as well as personal, costs. Bankruptcy, forged checks, theft, credit card debt, and prostitution all cost society, both in terms of unrecoverable debt and in terms of the legal costs incurred in processing crimes and bankruptcy. There are also social costs associated with pathological gambling that are more difficult to quantify, such as reduced productivity at work, unemployment, and the effects on children and the family structure.

Similar social costs are associated with kleptomania. In the United States, shoplifting may account for approximately $24 billion in business losses each year. Anywhere from 5 to 25 percent of shoplifters may suffer from kleptomania. Even using a conservative estimate of 5 percent who have kleptomania, however, one could argue that perhaps as much as $1.2 billion is lost from businesses each year as a result of this illness. When businesses lose money, society pays the price. This may be in the form of higher prices, reduced workforces, or reduced benefits for employees. Also, because of the personal difficulties associated with kleptomania, this disorder, like pathological gambling, often results in decreased work productivity, loss of employment, and negative effects on the family. These costs are larger than the individual costs, and they indirectly affect society.

There is not much evidence concerning the social costs of compulsive sexual behavior or compulsive shopping, but based upon our clinical experience, we often see similar social repercussions with these illnesses. People who suffer from impulse control disorders are often unable to work; they often lose their jobs, need hospitalization, and require long-term disability services. In the case of compulsive shopping, people suffering from this disorder, like pathological gamblers, often have severe financial problems as a result of credit card debt.

Impulse control disorders greatly affect the individuals suffering from them, but there are also tremendous social costs associated with these illnesses. Finding effective treatments, therefore, is not only in the best interest of the individuals but also in the interest of society.

5

Age and Gender: Influences on Impulse Control Disorders

"I've Been Doing This Since I Was a Kid": Children with Impulse Control Disorders

Now eleven years old, Dawn began stealing when she was only eight. "I started taking candy from the store. I don't know why. Since then I take all sorts of things. I can't stop myself." Dawn's mother explained that her daughter had been stealing peculiar items over the years—headbands, keys, nail clippers—and hoarding them in her closet. "She has boxes and boxes of silly things she has stolen. When I ask her why she took them, she cries. I think she's really scared about what she's doing, but she doesn't seem to be able to describe why." Although Dawn was outgoing, her mother reported that she often found Dawn crying in her room at night. When asked why, Dawn responded, "Only bad people steal stuff."

Rupert was nine years old when he began gambling with his eighteen-year-old brother. His mother described Rupert's behavior:

"His brother got him started. He always wanted to play poker, and he used to force Rupert into playing. After a while, however, Rupert was teaching kids at school the game and was taking their money. You can imagine how upset the teacher and the other parents were. I got calls for days telling me Rupert had a problem. At first I thought they were exaggerating, but I later realized he did have a problem. He began stealing money from my purse to gamble at school. When I forbid him to gamble, he gets so angry—in a way I have never seen before. And he cries when I stop him from gambling. I definitely think he has a problem."

When asked why he liked to play poker, Rupert replied, "It's cool. I like winning money from the other guys."

"What about when you lose?" I asked.

"I hate losing. I get pretty upset." I asked Rupert about stealing money. "I don't know why I did that. Sometimes I just do things. I guess I just wanted to gamble real bad. I'm not sure why I did it."

Although these cases show that impulse control disorders can exist in children, there is nothing in the medical literature that tells us how common impulse control disorders are among this age group. One of these disorders, compulsive sexual behavior, is not developmentally relevant to children. Another disorder, compulsive shopping, relies heavily upon having the independence to shop on one's own and thus is also not especially relevant to childhood. It is not unheard of for pathological gambling to begin in late childhood, but it appears to be relatively rare in this age group. Of all the disorders discussed here, kleptomania is perhaps the most frequently encountered among children.

Although stealing is common in children, obviously not all children who steal have kleptomania. In fact, among twenty-two people with kleptomania followed in our clinic, only three began stealing during childhood; most started in adolescence.

Children with impulse control disorders, particularly kleptomania, can vary in their presentation depending upon their stage of cognitive and emotional development. For example, for very young children, hoarding stolen items may function as a self-soothing mechanism. Also, children will vary as to whether they see their behavior as a problem. In older children, stealing may evoke very strong feelings of guilt and shame, and these children may strongly desire to stop the behavior. Do children outgrow such behavior? Although in many cases these are probably temporary behaviors that will disappear with time, no definitive answers are possible. There is, unfortunately, no research on very young people with these disorders or on the course of the disorders in this age group.

Because of the paucity of research in this area, there are no established standards of care for this age group. While it is certainly worth obtaining a professional consultation for children with these behaviors, successful treatment of such children requires an individualized treatment plan. Although studies on children with these problems are lacking, behavioral approaches should probably be tried before medication when treating children. The triggers for stealing must be explored in order to develop an effective behavior program; this may include understanding the situation that is giving rise to the behavior and, in older children, the emotions and thoughts associated with the behavior. Involvement of parents is also a key component in treating children with these behaviors. Engaging the child in alternative activities at high-risk times or providing alternatives to sensation stimulation or soothing behaviors may be necessary. The use of rewards may also be incorporated into the behavioral treatment.

"I Know There's Something Wrong with Me": Impulse Control Disorders among Adolescents

Impulse control disorders in adolescents may differ from those seen in children and may instead appear similar to the presentation we see in adults. Unlike the situation with children, who may display temporary behaviors, when adolescents display behaviors typical of an impulse control disorder, those behaviors are more likely to become persistent habits. Adolescents have greater access to money, and therefore, in addition to the stealing that we more commonly see in children, compulsive shopping and pathological gambling are more likely to develop at this period. Because of puberty, compulsive sexual behavior may also become a problem at this age.

In fact, most of the impulse control disorders begin in adolescence or early adulthood. The psychiatric literature has demonstrated fairly consistently that pathological gambling often starts in adolescence. In a sample of twenty-two kleptomaniacs that we treated, the average age at which stealing behavior became compulsive was approximately sixteen. Most of the people we treat for compulsive sexual behavior also report that they felt the behavior was "out of control" in late adolescence. People at this age appear to be particularly vulnerable to the development of these illnesses, and yet very little is known about these disorders in adolescents.

Do people who develop impulse control disorders at an early age differ from those with later onset of these disorders? In many psychiatric disorders, earlier onset often means more impairment, as the person suffers from the disorder for a longer period of time. Our clinical experience of these disorders suggests that the presentation of these disorders in adolescence appears similar to that seen in adults, with the degree of severity and of impairment ranging from mild to severe.

I met Graham, an eighteen-year-old man, when he was admitted to the hospital after discussing suicide with a friend. His parents had requested that I see him because he had been stealing for four years. Graham was noticeably embarrassed about discussing his stealing. "I've been doing it so long, I don't think about it anymore. I used to try to stop. I know it bothers my parents. And I know it's wrong, but other kids do it."

"Do you think the stealing has anything to do with your desire to kill yourself?" I asked.

"I know there's something wrong with me. Why would I do something I don't want to unless I'm either screwed up or just a really bad person? Either way, I know of only one solution to the problem." Upon further interviews, it was apparent that Graham was thinking about his behavior for several hours every day—that a combination of urges to steal and obsession with past behavior was causing him severe distress and was the cause of his depressed mood and suicidal thoughts.

It also became clear that Graham had wanted help for this problem for the past four years. "How could I tell my parents what I do? It's embarrassing. What were my options? Tell my parents they have a thief in the house or tell them they have a crazy son."

"But you feel incapable of stopping yourself," I responded.

"Who would believe that? As a thief I have zero credibility." Graham finally talked with his parents when he was apprehended for theft. "And now that my parents think I have a mental illness, they treat me like I'm going to do weird things at any moment. They act different around me. I think it may have been easier to have them believe I was a criminal."

Tina is another adolescent with an impulse control disorder — in her case, compulsive shopping. Tina's mother brought sixteen-year-old Tina to my office. Tina was obviously reluctant to tell her story. "Is this difficult for you to talk about?" I asked.

"Yes. I can't believe I have some illness. I mean, I knew maybe I had a problem, but I didn't think I needed a shrink."

"Why did you think you had a problem?" I asked.

"My mom gave me a credit card last year. At first I was really responsible with it. I don't really like to shop all that much, but sometimes with friends I would buy a few things. It got out of hand pretty quickly, though. I started buying lots of stupid things I didn't really want—I just wanted to buy something. Then the bill was getting huge. I had a deal with my parents that I would pay the bill. I didn't even want to show it to my parents. I couldn't even make the minimum payment, and yet I continued to shop. Shirts and sweaters I never wore. Books I didn't even want to read. I also started skipping school to go to the mall, alone. I didn't even want to hang out with my friends."

Tina was unable to talk with her parents about her problem. "I thought they'd think I was irresponsible. They trusted me with this card, and I had created a real mess. I was ashamed. Other kids had credit cards and hadn't gone crazy with them. I also thought I could stop on my own. I never knew it was something wrong with my brain." When her schoolwork began to suffer, Tina decided to talk with her parents. After hearing a local news show discuss compulsive shopping, Tina's parents brought her to our clinic. Tina responded well to medication and started seeing friends and doing well in school again.

There are numerous difficulties in diagnosing impulse control disorders in adolescents. One reason is that impulse control disorders often begin gradually, with a person feeling distressed and suffering functional impairment perhaps only after years of engaging in the behavior. Thus, adolescents may not recognize that what they are dealing with is the early manifestation of a behavioral addiction. Another reason for the difficulty in diagnosing these illnesses is an age-related reluctance to disclose concerns about problems with self-control. Adolescents are often secretive with adults. They may hesitate before confiding in adults, even (or perhaps especially) their parents. Disclosing information about one's lack of control over one's behavior—especially when the behavior has such shame attached—may therefore be particularly challenging for an adolescent. For parents, the best approach for discovering such behaviors is simply to ask when there are grounds for suspicion.

We are sometimes asked whether some impulse control disorders can even be diagnosed in adolescence because some impulsive behaviors are easily confused with normal adolescent development. For example, during adolescence, many people become obsessed with having sex. This "obsession" with sex may simply be part of normal maturation. However, when adolescents are using sex as a way of escaping from loneliness or feelings of inadequacy or when the behavior is causing problems, then it is not merely normal developmental behavior.

Virginia was seventeen years old when she began having sexual relationships. When she was not attending high school, Virginia would spend hours looking for a potential partner. Although initially embarrassed, Virginia was able to describe her sexual behavior. "I feel pretty stressed most of the time. Sex allows me to relax. I don't love the guys or anything like that. It's more that I need someone at the time." As further interviews would reveal, Virginia suffered from low self-esteem. For Virginia, sex became a means of managing stress and her self-defeating thoughts. During the time Virginia was left untreated, she experienced multiple sexually transmitted diseases and one unwanted pregnancy.

Although severe forms of impulse control disorders can easily be diagnosed in this age group, many mild cases of these disorders are difficult to differentiate from normal adolescent behavior. Alex began gambling on sporting events with friends at the age of sixteen. Alex and his friends would get together on weekends, bet on sporting events, and talk about school. Although his gambling did not cause difficulties in his peer relations, he did have some financial problems secondary to his gambling, and he became somewhat preoccupied with each week's wagers. Although Alex is perhaps not currently suffering from pathological gambling, his behavior could develop into a more severe problem over the next few years. Because adolescence appears to be the time when impulse control disorders are most likely to develop, an adolescent such as Alex should be closely followed to see if his behavior worsens.

Adolescents who are suffering from impulse control disorders are also at high risk of having problems with substance abuse, and this becomes yet another reason to diagnose and treat impulse control problems as soon as they start. It is not always clear which came first—did the impulse control disorder cause the abuse of drugs or alcohol as a way of coping, or did the abuse of drugs or alcohol lead to more impulsive behavior? There are no easy answers to this question. Having seen hundreds of people with impulsive behavior in our clinical practices, however, we do know that approximately 30 to 40 percent of the people who report impulsive behavior beginning during adolescence also report substance abuse during this time period. One possible explanation is that the same genetic vulnerability that results in people developing an impulse control disorder also contributes to the development of a substance abuse problem.

What this means in terms of treating adolescents is that parents and mental health providers must continue to ask questions about drugs and alcohol when treating impulse control disorders.

The presence of an impulse control disorder may also have effects on the normal development of adolescents. The tasks of adolescent development include becoming autonomous of parents, developing peer relationships, establishing one's sexuality, and forming a stable self-image or identity. Impulse control disorders may adversely affect this development. For instance, shame is intrinsic to these disorders. That shame may interfere with the establishment of a stable sense of self or a healthy identity. Adolescents with these disorders may see themselves in terms of the disorder—as pathological gamblers or kleptomaniacs—or in moral terms—as "bad" or "immoral" people.

If left untreated, compulsive sexual behavior may lead to questions or doubts about sexuality. A person with compulsive sexual behavior may not develop a healthy sexual identity. A person with such a disorder may believe that his or her identity is essentially his or her sexual attractiveness or his or her ability to perform sexually. Compulsive sexual behavior may also affect the person's ability to develop monogamous, trusting intimate relationships.

Both the shame associated with these behaviors and the compulsive quality of the disorders often lead young people to withdrawal socially, spending more time on the behavior or coping with the embarrassment and shame. This social withdrawal may affect their ability to develop or maintain healthy relationships. Instead of attending social events with peers, an adolescent pathological gambler may spend her or his time looking for opportunities to gamble. An adolescent compulsive shopper may be too preoccupied with buying things to socialize with friends. How an impulse control disorder may affect adolescent development is not yet exactly clear, but the lack of normal peer relationships and difficulty in developing a healthy identity most likely result in a variety of other social and psychological problems in later life.

As in an adult, a diagnosis of an impulse control disorder in an adolescent should be made when the person has intense urges to engage in behavior or has preoccupations with a behavior, and when that behavior interferes with the person's daily functioning. Because adolescents may not be forthcoming about their behavior, parents or adults should be concerned when an adolescent has difficulty in school, isolates him- or herself from friends, or becomes depressed. Like adults, adolescents with impulse control disorders often feel isolated as a result of their behavior. They may believe that no one else suffers from such a problem. It is essential that adolescents know that they are not alone. Although we will discuss this in a later chapter, it is also important to recognize that medications and therapy are effective in treating adolescents with impulse control disorders.

If left untreated, impulse control disorders appear to be chronic conditions. Approximately 70 to 80 percent of the people we treat report that the symptoms of their impulse control disorder have been continuous and chronic rather than episodic. That is, they do not recall a period of a month or longer when they were free of the symptoms, particularly the urges associated with their behavior. Although people may refrain from engaging in impulsive behavior, these same people will report that they rarely have several consecutive days when they do not feel urges to gamble, steal, have sex, or shop.

This is not to say that the symptoms of impulse control disorders do not wax and wane. In fact, although people may have few urge-free periods during the course of their illness, the urges and other symptoms are more severe at some times than at others. This change in symptom severity may coincide with stress (for example, financial, work, or family stress) or with emotional moments, or may fluctuate for no apparent reason.

Early treatment may reduce the severity of the disorder and may result in a shorter course of treatment. The adolescents described in this chapter responded to various medications (for example, selective serotonin reuptake inhibitors, opioid antagonists, and mood stabilizers) and to individual therapy. After several weeks or months of treatment, adolescents are able to resume normal functioning, establish relationships, and engage in fulfilling school and extracurricular activities. As with children, family involvement is particularly important when treating adolescents.

Impulse control disorders obviously occur in adolescents, perhaps even more than we are currently aware of. Shame, secrecy, and a lack of awareness on the part of parents and health-care providers most likely contribute to the difficulty that adolescents have in talking about these problems. But adolescents may in fact be particularly vulnerable to developing these disorders. Although more research is clearly needed in this area, the same treatments that are effective in adults appear to be effective in adolescents with these disorders. Therefore, it is important for parents and physicians to recognize and treat these illnesses.

"I Can't Believe I Have This Problem at My Age": The Elderly and Impulse Control Disorders

If left untreated, impulse control disorders appear to be chronic. Therefore, as one might expect, these disorders are not uncommon among the elderly. Although we often think of the elderly as being less impulsive, there is no clear evidence that these disorders "burn out" as one ages. In fact, in our clinic we treat many elderly patients who suffer from kleptomania, pathological gambling, and compulsive shopping. We have, however, seen far fewer elderly people suffering from compulsive sexual behavior. The reasons for this are not clear.

Yvonne, an eighty-two-year-old woman, sought treatment for compulsive shopping. "I think I've had this problem for probably forty years. I shop a lot because it makes me feel good. Even if I don't need or want the things, I still feel better when I'm shopping.

While my husband was working, it didn't cause any problems. After we retired, we had a fixed income. My shopping didn't change, however. I just can't control myself. You would think it would get old or I'd get tired of shopping so much, but it feels the same now as it did forty years ago. I've spent a lot of our savings, and my children are very upset with me. I'm really here because of them. They won't talk to me until I get help. I don't want them to be ashamed of me."

The elderly people that we see fall into two groups: those, like Yvonne, who have suffered from their illness for many years and those who develop an impulse control problem in their later years. In our experience, the presentation of these disorders appears fairly similar in these two groups. One difference is that people who have had a disorder for years often report less intense urges to behave in a certain way and instead refer to the behavior as a habit. Those elderly people who have recently developed an impulse control disorder, however, usually report intense urges to engage in certain behaviors, much like younger people with these disorders. Why do some people develop the problem early in their lives, while others seem to have the problem later? Is there a difference in what is happening in the brains of these two groups? The difference between these two groups may be a race between the activities of the frontal lobe and those of the basal region of the brain. If frontal lobe activities deteriorate faster than those of the basal brain region, impulsive behavior may emerge in later life. This may be further complicated by other illnesses. In diabetes or central nervous system vascular diseases, the ability of the frontal lobe to inhibit subcortical regions may weaken, also producing impulsive behavior. These are merely speculations, and we will discuss possible causes of impulse control disorders in Chapter 7. More research is obviously needed to address these questions.

The following case illustrates an impulse control disorder that started when the patient was already elderly. I first met Albert, a seventy-eight-year-old man, when he came to our clinic for treatment of pathological gambling. "I never gambled until two years ago. I decided to go to the casino with friends. I was hooked almost instantly. I don't know what happened. I've never had a problem with drugs or alcohol. I've never done anything addictive. Now I've lost savings, friends, and even my family because of my obsession with gambling. I can't believe I have this problem at my age." Albert had gone from recreational gambling to pathological gambling within one year of starting to gamble. He suffered almost daily from intense urges to gamble. He had little ability to resist these urges. As a result, the gambling had caused him serious financial, emotional, and social difficulties.

When Albert initially came to our clinic, he received a detailed medical examination. When an elderly person develops an impulse control disorder, it is important to make sure it is not due to some underlying medical condition. Dementia, disturbances in the electrolytes in a person's blood, and various tumors of the brain have all been associated with the development of impulse control disorders.

Elderly people with impulse control disorders, regardless of age of onset, look essentially the same as younger people with these disorders. In many illnesses, an earlier age of onset often predicts worse impairment in functioning. This does not appear to be the case with impulse control disorders. In fact, elderly people who develop the problem in later life seem to be as impaired as their younger counterparts, if not more so. Many of these individuals have never coped with a problem such as this at any time in their lives. To have to deal with the distress of these behaviors, as well as the social and financial difficulties that result, is often overwhelming for elderly people. Having lived for many years without a behavioral addiction, elderly people may also have more intense guilt and shame associated with their behaviors than younger people.

Elderly people with impulse control disorders also resemble younger people with these disorders in their response to treatment. In our experience, elderly people with these disorders appear to respond as well and as quickly as younger people. In fact, many elderly people with impulse control disorders may find relief at slightly lower doses of medication than those used with younger people. Elderly people with impulse control disorders also appear to respond as favorably as younger people to cognitive behavior therapy.

Little research has been done on how impulse control disorders change over the course of the illness. Long-term prospective studies that follow people over a long period are lacking. Will the untreated adolescent with an impulse control disorder look the same when he is elderly? Do elderly people with impulse control disorders cope better than younger people because they have dealt with their illness over a longer period of time, or do the years of having an untreated illness produce a cumulative effect of suffering? Are some treatments more effective in the elderly than they are in adolescents? Further research is needed to answer these important questions more definitively.

Men, Women, and Impulse Control Disorders: Differences and Similarities

Are impulse control disorders more common in men or in women? Do impulse control disorders look different in women and in men? Does gender affect how someone responds to treatment? Different impulse control disorders generate different answers to these questions.

Ben, a forty-five-year-old man, and Gail, his forty-two-year-old wife, sought treatment together for pathological gambling. Ben had started gambling in his early twenties. He now gambled approximately two or three times per week, playing blackjack at a local casino. Although he had been working in construction for years, the gambling had taken a toll on his job performance. Staying late at the casino had frequently made him late for work. Thoughts of "winning big" preoccupied him during the day, causing his concentration at work to suffer. Ben usually went to the casino with Gail. Although she preferred to play the slot machines, she was no less intense in her gambling than Ben. In fact, after eight or ten hours at the casino, it was often Ben who had to force Gail to leave. Gail worked in accounts at a large company, and she too found that her work was suffering because of the gambling—urges to gamble often intruded into her daily activities.

Ben and Gail had a seventeen-year-old son who was currently a senior in high school. Both Ben and Gail felt that they had ignored their son and his school activities because of their gambling. "He's going off to college next year, and this is our last intense period of time with him," Ben began. "But we'd rather spend our free time at the casino than with our son. He recently had a gymnastics tournament at school. He even received some type of medal. But we missed it. Actually, we just chose to ignore it so we could go to the casino."

"What kind of parents are we?" Gail asked and then started to cry. "I'm his mother, and I would prefer to lose money in a slot machine than share his high school moments. If this gambling continues, I know we'll lose him. I also know we'll have no one but ourselves to blame."

It has been assumed that pathological gambling is more common in men than in women. In fact, the ratio of male pathological gamblers to female pathological gamblers is believed to be approximately 2:1. This finding has been based on a few epidemiological studies. In clinical settings, however, this may be different. Our clinic probably sees more women than men who are seeking help for pathological gambling. Why should more females be coming to us for treatment? It may simply reflect a greater tendency of women with pathological gambling to seek treatment for their gambling problem. Perhaps it is easier to bring an ill female relative to a mental health facility than to bring an ill male relative—this is true with other psychiatric illnesses, such as manic-depressive illness. Or maybe our society has different expectations of normative behavior for men and women. Thus, people, including the addicted person, may feel that a woman with a gambling addiction needs help more than a man with the same problem.

The available data unfortunately are not adequate to give us as valid an estimate of the sex ratio of pathological gambling as we'd like. Larger epidemiological studies are needed to address this question. Until more information is available, all we can say with certainty is that pathological gambling affects both men and women.

Are there differences in men and women with pathological gambling? Our research has come up with answers to this question, and the professional literature tends to agree with our findings. For one thing, men tend to develop the illness at an earlier age than women. Whereas men may develop a problem with gambling in their mid-twenties, women may not report a problem until their early thirties. However, women appear to develop a pathological gambling problem over a shorter period from when they start gambling than men do.

We have also found that the types of gambling behavior differ between the sexes. Men are more likely to play blackjack, bet on sporting events, and bet on card games: They prefer the interactive forms of gambling. Women, on the other hand, choose less interactive forms of gambling—slot machines and bingo. Whereas both men and women most often have their gambling urges triggered by sensory stimuli (for example, advertisements or billboards), women tell us that their gambling behavior is also often triggered by feeling lonely or sad, having thoughts of winning, or being bored.

The severity of the illness and the degree of impairment (for example, marital or work problems, legal difficulties), appear to be similar in men and women. There are, however, differences in exactly how gambling has affected men and women. In terms of legal difficulties, among people we treat, 42 percent of the women and 39 percent of the men report a legal problem as a result of gambling difficulties, and 25 percent of women and 19 percent of men report committing an illegal act because of their gambling. Women are three times more likely to report writing bad checks knowingly. Men, on the other hand, are more likely to report that they lost their savings, their homes, or their cars or pawned items because of gambling. Also, a greater number of men than women report having taken out bank loans to cover gambling debts, and men are more likely to commit tax fraud because of their gambling.

Male and female pathological gamblers often have similar family histories with respect to problematic gambling and alcohol use. Of the people we have treated, approximately one-third of both men and women had a father with problematic gambling behavior, and approximately one-fourth of both male and female pathological gamblers had a mother with problematic gambling behavior. With respect to alcohol use, approximately one-half of both men and women report that their fathers suffered from an alcohol problem. Also, about 10 percent of both men and women report that their mothers suffered from an alcohol problem.

The male and female pathological gamblers that we treat are largely similar in terms of coexisting psychiatric disorders (for example, depression), although some studies suggest that alcohol or drug use is more common in male pathological gamblers. Also, men and women appear to respond equally well both to medications and to cognitive behavior therapy.

Gender issues in kleptomania are just beginning to be explored. The literature has been fairly consistent in finding that the majority of people who suffer from kleptomania—perhaps as much as 70 percent—are females. This finding, however, may be biased by the very small number of people who have been treated for kleptomania and by those who seek treatment for this problem. Perhaps more men suffer from kleptomania than we are aware of, but they do not seek treatment from physicians or therapists. In fact, our clinic probably receives an equal number of telephone calls from males and females seeking treatment for stealing behavior. It is not possible to say how many of the calls we receive are from people who suffer from kleptomania, but the number of calls suggests that more people may have this disorder than are willing to come for treatment. This may also suggest that women are more likely to actually come to a physician's office than men are.

Are there gender differences in kleptomania? The number of people, particularly men, who come to the attention of physicians has simply been too small to make meaningful distinctions based on gender. Looking at our clinic population, there do not seem to be any differences between male and female kleptomaniacs in terms of items stolen, severity of illness, related psychiatric illnesses, or problems resulting from their behavior. Both male and female kleptomaniacs suffer intense guilt and shame secondary to their behavior. Also, both sexes have responded equally well to available treatments for kleptomania. In upcoming years, as more research is done on kleptomania, it will be important to continue to examine gender differences in this disorder.

Compulsive shopping also appears to be a disorder that affects females disproportionately (perhaps as many as 80 percent of people suffering from this disorder are women). Although there is some suggestion that male compulsive shoppers may purchase larger, more expensive items, there is not enough evidence to make statements regarding gender differences in this disorder. As in the case of kleptomania, most of the people seeking treatment for compulsive shopping tend to be women. Whether there are an equal number of men with this disorder who simply suffer in silence is currently not known.

On the other hand, compulsive sexual behavior appears to affect males more often than females. Like pathological gambling, compulsive sexual behavior may simply be a more socially defined urge-driven behavior in males than in females. Some researchers have suggested that males may be socialized to be more sexually aggressive and visually focused. Therefore, it may not be surprising that more men than women would identify themselves as compulsively sexual.

In our experience, the impulse control disorders, with the exception of pathological gambling, do not present differently between the sexes. Males and females with these illnesses suffer the distress and the consequences equally. Statements regarding gender differences in these disorders are based on relatively small numbers of people. Additionally, even the sex ratios seen in these disorders may in fact reflect cultural biases more than gender differences in brain neural circuitry and functioning. For example, in Western culture, sex is defined largely from a male perspective. Conversely, shopping has historically been largely the domestic sphere of women. Can this explain why women have been willing to seek treatment for compulsive shopping, whereas men more often tell their physicians about compulsive sexual behavior? The answer may be much more complicated.

Is the neural circuit in the brain that appears to be responsible for all urge-based disorders different in men and women? Why are men more likely to gamble and have sex and women more likely to steal and shop? The issue of gender in impulse control disorders is still being explored. As these disorders and various treatments are researched, the issue of gender should continue to be examined.

6

Why People Behave Impulsively

Not All Impulsive Behavior Is Alike: Subtypes and Implications for Treatment

People who suffer from impulse control disorders are not all alike, even when they have the same disorder. For example, the psychological or emotional reasons for compulsive gambling will differ between individual gamblers. Two compulsive shoppers may give very different reasons for what motivates their shopping. In fact, if one looks at the motivational drives of people with impulse control disorders, there are probably three subtypes: people whose behavior is secondary to urges, those who engage in behavior because of their emotional state (usually feeling dysphoric), and those whose impulsive behavior is generated by a combination of urges and emotions. Although urges are the distinguishing feature of these disorders, a small percentage of people do not report urges.

The first type consists of people who behave impulsively because they have urges to engage in certain behaviors. Many people with an impulse control disorder report having urges or cravings to engage in the specific behavior, such as gambling or shopping. These urges are often triggered by certain specific environmental cues—for example, certain visual cues or sounds, or having the means to engage in the behavior (for compulsive shoppers or gamblers, extra money). People in this subgroup may look a lot like many people who suffer from alcohol or drug addiction and who describe cravings even when they are not using substances. Of the people with impulse control disorders that we treat, approximately 50 percent report urges as the driving force behind their behavior.

The second type includes people who engage in impulsive behavior because of their emotional state. Many people with an impulse control disorder report that the way they feel—sad, lonely, bored, anxious—determines whether they will engage in certain behaviors. For example, some people compulsively shop or have sex only when they feel lonely or bored. They may describe the behavior as an "escape" from the way they feel emotionally. These people do not identify urges as the source of their impulsive behaviors. This subtype of impulse control disorder also has a parallel with substance abusers, as many people who suffer from alcoholism report drinking to escape loneliness or depression. This subtype probably accounts for approximately 10 percent of the people we treat.

And finally, about 40 percent of our patients do not fit neatly into either of these groups and therefore represent a combined subtype of impulse control disorders. These people report urges to engage in behavior, but the urges may be prompted by the person's emotional state. For example, a person suffering from kleptomania may say that she has urges to steal, but that these urges are triggered only when she is feeling lonely. The loneliness is an emotional state from which the stealing allows a person to "escape" and also a trigger for cravings or urges to steal. This subtype of people who suffer from impulse control disorders is important because it has implications for treatment. For some people, the urge must be treated, whereas in others the mood state should be addressed. We will discuss treatment in Chapter 8.

"I Can't Stop Myself": The Urges behind Impulse Control Disorders

People with impulse control disorders usually describe fairly specific triggers for their urges. For example, the majority of pathological gamblers report that advertisements such as those on television or radio, having extra money or time, and the possibility of winning are the primary triggers of urges. People with kleptomania report that the sights and sounds of stores or the thoughts of certain objects will trigger urges. Compulsive shoppers may find that television advertisements prompt their cravings, while people with compulsive sexual behavior cite media representations of people with attractive bodies as the most frequent force behind their urges. Some people, however, have no identifiable triggers for their urges.

Paul, a forty-two-year-old physician, reported shopping daily in response to urges. "When I watch television or read magazines and see houses with certain furniture or various household items, I have these intense urges to buy something. The urges consume my whole body. I can feel the cravings in my gut and in my bones. At times the urges are so strong they actually cause my muscles to hurt. The urges also fill my thoughts. When I have an urge, it's all I can think about. I don't need the items I buy. In fact, my house is beautifully furnished already. But I probably shop almost every day because of these urges. If I don't shop, the urges disrupt my concentration and I can't function. It seems the only way to relieve the urges is to shop."

Jennifer, a twenty-one-year-old college student, sought treatment in our clinic because of stealing. "I sit in class, and I will have an overwhelming urge to steal something. Suddenly, no matter what is going on in class, I can't think of anything but stealing. The urge to steal is so strong. It's as if something else is driving my thoughts and behavior. I don't want to steal, but I get this feeling deep in my stomach that I have to. The urges completely preoccupy me until either I give in to them or they go away. If I try to resist, the urges seem to get worse—they're so uncomfortable. It's usually just easier and quicker to give in."

Because urges are often associated with certain triggers, many people avoid the triggers in order to prevent the behavior. For some people, however, avoidance of the trigger either may not be possible or may result in severe social or occupational dysfunction because of the character of the trigger. Megan, a forty-three-year-old mother and housewife, suffered from kleptomania. Whenever she entered a store, she would have intense urges to steal something. She was terrified by the idea of being apprehended: "If the police ever caught me, especially when I am with my children, I don't think I could go on living." Because stores triggered the urges to steal, Megan chose not to shop. Although she had always done the shopping both for groceries and for things for the children, Megan turned that responsibility over to her husband. "I told him that he could do the shopping. The problem was that I didn't tell him why. He had never known about my stealing, and I didn't want him to know. He didn't understand why I wouldn't shop any longer, and it made him angry. He thought I just didn't want to help with the family. I would rather have him believe I'm lazy than know I'm a thief."

Nick reported that billboards triggered his urges to gamble. Coming home past a billboard for a local casino would often cause him to drive to the casino instead of to his home. "I wouldn't even be thinking about gambling when I started driving home. And then I'd see that billboard, and the urges just flooded me. Although my wife wanted me to come home, going home seemed unimportant." In order to save his marriage, Nick planned several alternative routes home so that he could avoid the billboard. He was able to prevent having urges by avoiding the trigger.

For some people, the urges to engage in impulsive behavior may not be linked to an identifiable trigger. "I don't know where my urges come from," answered Laura, a twenty-nine-year-old woman who came to our clinic for kleptomania. "I know I wake up in the morning with these urges. Nothing seems to be going through my mind at that time. I wish there was a trigger—I could just avoid it. But I don't know what my trigger is, or if I even have one. The urges are intense. I thought they'd go away if I just avoided them— you know, tried to distract myself. They don't. I have gone days without stealing, and the urges just get more severe. When they become uncontrollable, I give in and steal something. I know I could quit this behavior if I could just get rid of the urges."

"My Gambling Allows Me to Escape": Depression, Boredom, and Anxiety

The second subtype of people with impulse control disorders may be thought of as those who engage in behavior because of the way they feel. About 10 percent of our patients report that they gamble/ shop/steal/have sex because they feel depressed, bored, or anxious. They deny that they have urges or that these mood states prompt cravings. They simply state that the impulsive behavior allows them to escape from their current mood. They may or may not have an independent mood disorder such as major depressive disorder or an anxiety disorder. Much like alcohol-dependent individuals who drink as a way to escape their problems, some people with impulse control disorders also appear to engage in the various behaviors as a means of escape.

Although approximately 30 to 40 percent of our patients have a lifetime mood disorder (for example, major depression or bipolar disorder) in addition to their impulse control disorder, many do not currently have an independent mood disorder, such as major depression. Even among those who do not, however, significant mood symptoms may still give rise to their impulsive behavior. It is not uncommon for people to report that the impulsive behavior allows them to escape their feelings of loneliness or boredom.

David, a fifty-eight-year-old widower, described how his mood affected his gambling behavior. "I usually go to the casino when I'm feeling lonely. I started to go as a way to escape my loneliness. The gambling has caused some serious financial problems for me—I've lost most of my retirement savings, and I have substantial credit card debt. But I can't imagine stopping. How would I deal with being alone? I have so little else in my life. I never socialize, and I have very few friends. Gambling allows me to escape my emptiness."

"I shop because I can escape the way I feel" was the way Samantha, a thirty-year-old single woman, described her shopping. "I don't think of myself as clinically depressed, but I have nothing else in my life that brings me such happiness. I look forward to going to the stores after work each day. For a few minutes each day, I feel special and not so down. I don't want the things I buy. I just enjoy the act of buying them. Sure it has caused financial difficulties for me—I can't even pay the minimums on my credit cards—but it also has brought me a lot of joy."

Leah described her engaging in sexual activity with multiple anonymous partners as resulting from boredom. "I have sex to escape the boredom of my life. I work as an attorney and live alone. I have very little in my life except my work—no hobbies and just a couple of friends who are always busy. I fundamentally believe my sexual behavior is immoral. I don't even want to do it—it merely fills some time. But it's also pretty exciting. The whole experience of meeting a stranger and then seeing if he'll sleep with me gets me excited. If I had other things to do, I doubt if I would behave this way. The problem is that it's starting to get in the way of my work. I'm preoccupied with sex—thinking about it when I should be working."

Although many people with impulse control disorders may have only mild symptoms of depression, some people do have more serious mood disorders. Some may suffer from major depressive disorder or bipolar disorder in addition to the impulse control disorder. We will discuss these problems in more depth in a later chapter. It is important that people who behave impulsively because of their emotions be screened for more serious mood disorders.

"I Have Urges to Shop When I Feel Stressed": Emotions and Urges

Finally, another group of people with impulsive behavior (about 40 percent of our patients) report that their emotional state and their urges are intertwined. This group belongs to the combined subtype of impulse control disorder, in which both emotions and urges generate behavior seemingly inseparably. Janie, an emergency room nurse, came to our clinic complaining of a problem with excessive shopping. "I have urges to shop when I've had a lousy day. When the job is stressful, I have these urges to buy things. I feel stress and anxiety, and suddenly these cravings start in my gut, and I can't resist them. So I shop on my way home. On weekends when I'm not working, however, I don't seem to have these urges. The problem is that I have more stressful days than relaxing ones."

This connection between emotions and urges may result in a complex cycle of behavior in which it is difficult to determine whether the urge or the emotion is primary. Wayne, a twenty-seven-year-old who suffers from pathological gambling, describes the complexity of his behavior: "I think I started gambling because of feeling down. When I go home after work, and I feel sad or that my life is empty, I get these urges to gamble. The urges are intense, and I usually can't resist them. When I come home from the casino, I'm even more depressed—usually because I'm a lot poorer. For the next few days, I'm pretty depressed about my life. The problem is that this depression also causes me to have urges to gamble more. It's a vicious cycle. The more I gamble, the more depressed I get, and the more I have urges to gamble." Wayne responded well to both an antidepressant and naltrexone, an "anti-urge" medication. People who experience urges as a result of strong emotions need to have both the urge and the emotional state treated.

"I Gamble When I Drink": Alcohol Use and Impulse Control Disorders

One final category involves people who engage in impulsive behavior under the influence of substances. For example, alcohol use plays a complicated role in impulse control disorders. In our clinical experience, alcohol appears to have no significant role in compulsive shopping or kleptomania. It is, however, a factor in compulsive sexual behavior and pathological gambling. Does alcohol use cause people to gamble or have sex more? Or does the gambling or the sexual problem lead to more alcohol use? There are no simple answers to these questions.

Kevin, a forty-one-year-old cashier, described his use of alcohol while gambling: "I go to the casino about two or three times each week. I drink only rarely when I'm not at the casino. I probably drink once a month at the casino. On the nights I drink, I gamble a lot more. I also probably play for higher stakes when I drink. I think the drinking causes me not to worry about my gambling, and so I'm more likely to make bad bets."

Our research has shown that about one-fourth to one-third of our pathological gamblers have had a problem with alcohol use at some time in their lives. Although alcohol is often served in gambling establishments, many pathological gamblers report that alcohol blunts their ability to think carefully about their betting, and so they abstain from its use while they are gambling. Instead, most of our patients smoke at the casinos, reporting that nicotine "sharpens" their thinking. These people may, however, drink after a night of losing at the casino. "I only drink after losing at the casino," Randall told me. "Sometimes I drink a lot to just help me forget what I've done." Whether alcohol use actually contributes to gambling behavior is still unclear.

"I'm Not Sure I Want to Stop": The Rewards of Impulse Control Disorders

Although the urges behind impulsive behavior are often described as uncontrollable, many people do not resist these urges because there is a clear reward for the behavior. In fact, the impulsive behavior itself may actually be pleasurable. This is particularly true early in the course of the various illnesses. Given this reward aspect, impulse control disorders often produce a great conflict in the people who suffer from them. Most people who suffer from impulse control disorders experience urges to engage in behavior that they know results in social, occupational, or personal difficulties. In most cases, however, it is the consequences of the behavior that are troubling, not the behavior itself. These consequences are usually the reasons people seek treatment.

Denise, a twenty-eight-year-old mother of three, sought help in our clinic for compulsive sexual behavior. "I just can't resist the urges," Denise began, with tears in her eyes. "I started having these urges about six years ago. I thought they'd go away either as I got older or after I got married, but they haven't. In fact, I think they've actually become more severe over the last couple of years. I work. I raise my children. I love my husband, and we have a good sex life. But this other side of me I can't control."

"Can you describe the urges?" I asked.

"I have urges to have sex with anonymous men. The urges are sort of like cravings. I used to use cocaine in my early twenties, and these cravings are exactly the same. I have urges probably every day, but they are usually mild and I can resist acting on them. Probably about once a week, however, I get a severe urge that I can't resist, no matter how hard I try to distract myself. Usually I have the severe urges when I'm feeling stressed about work or the kids."

Although she had experienced these urges for approximately six years, Denise had never sought treatment prior to coming to our clinic. "It was only recently that my husband found out. He's threatened to leave me and take our children unless I get help."

"Do you want help?" I asked.

"I'm not sure," Denise answered and then burst into tears. "Don't get me wrong. I don't want to lose my husband or my children. I love them all so much. But I also enjoy this behavior. It's exciting. It makes me feel alive. I just don't want to feel out of control or have problems because of it. I guess I would like to know if I can just have better control over my behavior. I know some people with alcoholism who still drink—they just do it responsibly. Can I do that with my sexual behavior?"

"People who come to see you probably want to stop stealing, right?" Brian asked as he took a seat in my office. "I'm not sure I want to. I enjoy stealing—I get something for nothing, and the act of stealing relieves my anxiety. What I don't enjoy are the cravings I get and the guilt I have after I've taken something." I asked him to describe his cravings. "I wake up in the morning and have these urges to steal something. I usually try to resist them, and they may go away—at least for a while. When the urges are more intense, they won't go away no matter what I do. I start feeling really anxious—like I'm going to explode. The one thing that relieves the anxiety is stealing. At first I was taking anything—even silly things like cigarette lighters or nail polish. Over the years, however, I realized that I might as well take things I could use. Now I steal things I want.

"Am I just a common thief?" Brian asked. He looked distraught as he formulated an answer to his own question, "I used to think I was, but I realize I have an illness. I can't resist these urges to steal— I'm not in control. I may take things I want, but I suffer because of it. I know right from wrong, and I know what I'm doing is wrong. I've tried to kill myself twice because of the guilt I feel. The problem is that the stealing makes me feel better for a little while, and so I have mixed feelings about it."

The enjoyment of impulsive behavior is also seen in cases of pathological gambling. Julie, a thirty-one-year-old bank teller, described her urges to gamble and the feelings associated with gambling: "I have intense urges to gamble every time I see a television advertisement for a local casino. I can be watching television and not thinking about gambling until a commercial comes on. Then I have to get to the casino no matter what. If anyone tries to stop me, I can be a real bitch. The urges are so strong. But I also enjoy gambling. It's exciting—the lights, the noise, all the people. Also, I often win, and there's nothing more exciting than winning. Even winning a few dollars is a thrill. I don't always win, however. When I lose, I'm not so fond of gambling. Sometimes I wish I could stop. What I probably mean is that I wish I could stop losing. Do I have a mental disorder if I like the behavior but sometimes hate the outcome?"

Many people with impulse control disorders enjoy their behavior, at least to some extent. For example, a pathological gambler may enjoy the excitement and the "rush" from going to a casino, and more specifically from winning. Many people with kleptomania report excitement from stealing and not getting caught. Compulsive shoppers report a thrill from buying excessive amounts of merchandise. Of all the people with impulse control disorders that we have interviewed, approximately 70 to 90 percent report getting some enjoyment or excitement from their behavior, especially at the outset of the disorder. The great majority of these people describe this excitement as an integral part of their behavior early in the course of the illnesses.

This feeling of excitement leads many people to be unsure whether they want treatment for their disorders. The idea of medicating away the thrill of gambling is not appealing for many people. In fact, many people choose to stop taking their medication or going to therapy when they no longer have the urge to engage in the impulsive behavior. Ian, a thirty-year-old man who suffered from pathological gambling, described why he quit taking his medication: "When I was taking naltrexone, I had no urges to gamble. I also didn't enjoy gambling as much the times I did go to the casino. I used to enjoy the rush of going to the casino and playing blackjack. I know it caused a lot of problems, but it also brought me a lot of enjoyment. I quit taking the medication because I wanted to relive that thrill again. The thrill returned right after I quit taking the medication. The problems also came right back." Kyle, a person with compulsive sexual behavior, also stopped therapy and medication when they began to decrease the frequency of his sexual behavior. "I enjoyed it. When the treatment took it away from me, I missed it."

Because of the pleasurable aspects of impulsive behavior, many people do not seek treatment for their disorders or do not stay in treatment once therapy or medication appears to be effective. In our clinical experience, for every patient who seeks treatment, approximately eight others have contacted us seeking information about treatment. There are multiple reasons that people do not come forward for treatment—for example, distrust of medical professionals, family difficulties, or financial problems. Among the possible reasons, however, is the desire to retain behavior that is pleasurable. In addition, approximately 50 percent of people who do seek treatment do not continue in treatment. Again, many factors are responsible for people dropping out of treatment (for example, lack of insurance or difficulty finding time for appointments), but one factor that is difficult to address is the excitement that people lose when their behavior changes. Because these disorders often have a severe impact on family and friends, as well as on the person with the disorder, it is important for these people to seek and continue with treatment. Often focusing on how the illness affects family can counterbalance the thrill associated with the behavior.

People who seek treatment need to be reminded that treating the disorder allows them to replace old habits with new outlets. People tell us that they have more time, money, and energy once their disorder is treated. This allows them to engage more fully at work, to pursue recreational activities, to renew and improve relationships with their family, and to restore and strengthen social and community relations.

Furthermore, the feeling of excitement associated with impulse control disorders appears to change over time. In fact, the behavior often has to increase or change in some way in order for the person to achieve the same level of enjoyment. For example, the gambler may begin to bet with larger amounts of money, the kleptomaniac may steal more expensive items in places where apprehension is more likely, and the person with a compulsive sexual disorder may have more sexual relations in riskier situations. In time, however, the excitement seems to disappear altogether, and the person is left with urges that no longer result in a "high."

"I Don't Get a 'Rush' Anymore, but I Still Can't Stop": Urges without Reward

Often the thrill or excitement associated with impulse control disorders disappears with time, and all that remains is the urge to engage in the behavior without any reward from the behavior. Anthony, a forty-three-year-old pathological gambler, describes the course of his illness over the last ten years: "When I started gambling, it was thrilling. I had severe urges to gamble, but they didn't bother me because the act of gambling was so enjoyable. I would often win, but even when I didn't, the casino was still an exciting place to be. There was music, noise, lights, people—a lot of stimulation. The problem was that this changed over time." For Anthony, after about two years of gambling, the excitement seemed to disappear. "I noticed that when other people talked about a 'rush' or a 'thrill,' I no longer felt that. In fact, I was gambling only because I couldn't stop myself. I still have intense urges, but now I don't look for a thrill. Initially, I thought I needed to gamble with more money to get the thrill again. This worked at first, but even high stakes didn't produce the former excitement. For the past seven or eight years I have been gambling because I have to, not because I want to."

Lucille, a fifty-eight-year-old woman suffering from kleptomania, describes stealing for years without getting any excitement or "high" from the behavior. "I think it was exciting at first. By that I mean maybe thirty years ago. I remember getting a kick out of stealing something and not getting caught. I think I used to steal cuff links at first. The thrill didn't last long, however, and I had to steal more expensive things to keep getting a thrill. I also took odd items. I think I gradually started stealing jewelry and clothing that cost a lot. That also produced some excitement—but again, only for a little while. After that, it didn't seem to matter how expensive the items were—I just couldn't feel the 'high' from stealing any longer. I haven't felt that excitement for years, and yet I have continued to steal. All I feel is disgust with myself. I feel weak that I cannot resist these cravings I get almost every day. If you think I steal because I get some sort of charge out of it, let me disabuse you of that idea right now. I would do anything to stop stealing. I would miss nothing about this behavior if I could stop today."

Among the people who come to our clinic for treatment, the ones who have suffered from an impulse control disorder for many years are more likely to report either decreased urges or urges without the rewards, excitement, or thrills from their behavior. People who once reported intense urges may find that the severity of these feelings decreases with time. Instead of being "impulsive," the behavior becomes more "compulsive," more like a habit. Additionally, many people initially report that they increased the behavior over time in order to recapture the original thrill. In time, however, the excitement may disappear regardless of the frequency and intensity of the behavior. Although data on the longitudinal course of these disorders are lacking, the excitement from the behavior appears to decrease or even disappear altogether if a person has suffered from the disorder for more than five to ten years. After this time, urges or a person's emotional state often trigger the behavior without compensatory rewards. Because there may no longer be any rewards associated with the behavior after a number of years, people seeking treatment after having an impulse control disorder for several years are often more likely to be compliant with medication and therapy. Waiting years before seeking treatment, however, means that the consequences of the impulsive behavior tend to be more severe.

"If I Stop Gambling, Will I Start Drinking Again?": Shifting from One Disorder to Another

Many people we treat ask us if there is such a thing as an addictive personality. Will treatment simply stop one behavior while other impulsive activities take its place? Older literature on alcohol abuse warned treatment providers that recovering alcoholics must be watched for signs of developing gambling problems or other behaviors. In our clinical experience, this is not the case. For people who act impulsively as a result of urges, the treatment targets the urges for external rewards. There is no part of the brain that is the gambling center or the kleptomania center. Instead, as we discuss more thoroughly in Chapter 7, part of the brain processes urges for external rewards. When the person is treated properly, these pathological urges are extinguished. That means there are no urges for stealing, gambling, or alcohol. (This does not apply neatly to all urges, however. For instance, urges to overeat, smoke cigarettes, or use certain drugs appear to be processed somewhat differently from the urges in impulse control disorders or alcoholism.) Therefore, in our clinical work, we do not see pathological gamblers suddenly becoming kleptomaniacs or alcoholics.

In the case of those who engage in impulsive behavior as a result of a desire to escape the depression or anxiety that they feel, once the underlying depression or anxiety is treated, they, too, do not appear to engage in some new impulsive behavior. The desire to escape into impulsive behavior disappears when the depression or anxiety is properly treated.

No one with an impulse control disorder should avoid treatment out of fear that some other impulsive behavior will replace the current behavior. In fact, our clinical work suggests the opposite: When people suffer from two or more impulsive behaviors, they may in fact find that the same treatment relieves both of them. For example, Gordon, a fifty-one-year-old man, came to our clinic seeking treatment for kleptomania. Gordon also suffered from compulsive sexual behavior. "I thought it was too much to ask that both problems be fixed. At first I was just so relieved that I quit stealing. Then I realized that my sexual problem also was gone." Gordon was treated effectively with naltrexone, an opioid antagonist, for both disorders. Several years later, Gordon had not developed an additional impulse control disorder to replace the others.

7

Possible Causes of Impulse Control Disorders

The cause of impulse control disorders remains largely a mystery. There is, however, much speculation and theorizing about possible causes, ranging from neurobiological theories (for example, malfunctioning of various brain chemicals) to the psychological meanings behind various behaviors (for example, that women who steal are displaying repressed sexual feeling). Even social or cultural arguments have been proposed to explain impulse control disorders (for example, popular culture's insistence on having possessions causes compulsive shopping).

Do all impulse control disorders have the same cause? If so, why do certain people develop pathological gambling and others compulsively have sex? Most likely, the cause of impulse control disorders is a combination of all three factors: neurobiological, psychological, and sociocultural. In fact, the separation of various causal influences into these three distinct categories is somewhat artificial. These factors most probably interact in very complex ways, and separating them may be difficult or even impossible.

The Neurobiology of Impulse Control Disorders

Although the impulse control disorders have been recognized for centuries, until recently clinicians and researchers have paid little attention to the neurobiological underpinnings of these disorders. We will begin by considering the various neurochemical systems that may be involved in impulse control disorders and then discuss the neuroanatomic systems that may mediate these disorders.

Several chemicals in brain cells may be involved in the neurobiology of various unwanted behaviors. Serotonin is a brain chemical that works as a neurotransmitter. It carries messages from one nerve cell to another. When serotonin moves from one cell to another, it triggers various chemical reactions in the recipient nerve cell. This process results in a network of nerve cell reactions in the regions where serotonin moves among nerve cells that branch out throughout the brain. Serotonin plays an important role in depression, anxiety, and obsessive-compulsive symptoms, as well as in appetite, sleep, and cognition.

Abnormalities in the serotonin system may also contribute to the poorly controlled initiation and cessation of behaviors seen in people with impulse control disorders. Alice, a forty-five-year-old compulsive shopper, described her difficulties: "When I have thoughts of shopping, I have to go. Nothing seems to stop me. I also have problems leaving the store. It's as if I can't pull myself away from it." Low levels of platelet monoamine oxidase, thought to reflect serotoninergic function, have been reported in males with pathological gambling. Males with pathological gambling have also been shown to demonstrate differences from normal controls in behavioral and biochemical responses to the serotoninergic agents clomipramine and meta-chlorophenyl-piperazine (m-CPP). In fact, people with other types of impulsive behavior, such as alcoholics or those who compulsively pull their hair, have reported a "high" after receiving m-CPP. Low levels of the serotonin metabolite 5-hydroxyindoleacetic acid (5-HIAA) have been reported in the cerebrospinal fluid of people with impulsive characteristics.

Recent brain imaging studies have suggested that low serotonin function within the frontal part of the brain engenders disinhibited behaviors and may trigger the diverse impulse control disorders. As we discuss later, selective serotonin reuptake inhibitors (SSRIs) appear to have a role in the treatment of impulse control disorders.

Other neurotransmitters may also be involved in impulse control disorders. Dopamine is a neurotransmitter that is involved in disorders of thinking and movement. Abnormalities in dopamine metabolism may also underlie the problems with reward and reinforcement seen in people with impulse control disorders. Evidence suggests that specific genetically mediated variations in a dopamine receptor gene may produce, to some extent, individual differences in reward motivation and responsiveness. Other dopamine genes may be involved in human novelty-seeking behavior, which is often a personality feature of those with impulse control disorders. Addiction may be due to increased dopamine activity in a specific brain region (the mesocorticolimbic circuit) by mediating reward, motivation, and reinforcing aspects of behavior.

Finally, two other chemicals are also of interest in impulse control disorders. First, norepinephrine may mediate aspects of arousal, attention, and sensation seeking. Nicki, a person suffering from kleptomania, also reported a desire for other thrill-seeking behaviors. "I get a rush from stealing. I don't want to do it, but there is an excitement to it. I also enjoy white-water rafting and skydiving. I think they're all related in some way."

And second, endogenous opioids appear to mediate levels of pleasure and influence dopamine activity in various brain regions (the reward circuit), thereby affecting a person's urges or cravings.

Ronald, a thirty-five-year-old man who suffered from pathological gambling, discussed his reasons for gambling: "I get these urges to gamble that are so intense. I'm unable to resist them. I know this disease is in my brain. I'm doing things I don't want to. It's out of my control." Ronald was successfully treated with naltrexone, an opioid antagonist. As we later discuss, opioid receptor antagonists have been shown to be effective in reducing urges/cravings in people with impulse control disorders.

Are there specific circuits or functional brain systems that are involved in impulse control disorders? Multiple lines of evidence now suggest that perhaps impulse control disorders should be thought of as behavioral addictions. The brain appears to have a distinct reward circuitry, and this same pathway may be activated in drug abusers and those with impulse control disorders. When the reward for a behavior is potent enough, it may trigger an addiction to that behavior. The addictive behavior appears to overtake or control this reward circuitry. Thus, impulse control disorders involve the loss of voluntary control over behavior. Many people with impulse control disorders become like robots. They engage in behavior almost without conscious recognition of what they are doing. They become trapped in repetitious, self-defeating behavior.

Preclinical and clinical studies demonstrate that the underlying neurobiological mechanism of urge-based disorders may involve the processing of incoming reward inputs by the ventral tegmental area–nucleus accumbens–orbital frontal cortex circuit (VTA-NA-OFC, or the reward circuit) in the brain. This circuit then influences behavior by modulating motivation (for example, urges or cravings), both in animals and in humans. As stated previously, dopamine and endorphins may play a major role in the regulation of this region's functioning.

Neurobiology and behavior are further linked by recent scientific studies showing that repeatedly engaging in behaviors such as gambling, stealing, or using addictive drugs may lead to long-lasting changes in the brain. The brain seems to memorize detailed information associated with these behaviors and to begin to make this information a part of the permanent memory pool. These kinds of changes then lead to permanent or near-permanent structural changes in the brain. Once this happens, any object or event that was previously associated with the behavior (whether that behavior is gambling, stealing, or something else) will trigger an intense compulsion to engage in the behavior. It is as if the brain wants more and more of the same behavior and deprives the person of his or her personal willpower or conscious decision-making abilities. The brain has now adapted permanently to the excitement and pleasure in spite of the grave consequences. When people report feeling "out of control" with respect to their behavior, they may be correct—their brains may well be more in control of their behavior than their conscious decision-making abilities are.

Further support for a neurobiological basis for impulse control disorders may be found in reports of various brain injuries that have resulted in impulse control disorders. For example, kleptomania has been reported in people with dementia and decreased levels of neurotransmitters, in people with cortical atrophy, and in a person with a tumor in the parietal lobe of the brain. Similarly, compulsive sexual behavior has been noted in people with frontal lobe lesions, temporal lobe epilepsy, dementia, and cerebral vascular accidents. New-onset pathological gambling in elderly people may also be due to changes in brain function or structure. As we mentioned in Chapter 5, if frontal lobe activities deteriorate faster than those of the basal brain region, impulsive behavior may emerge in later life. This may explain various late-onset impulse control disorders.

Brain imaging techniques have greatly advanced the search for structural and functional abnormalities of the brain in various psychiatric disorders. Such studies are just getting underway in impulse control disorders. One study by Marc Potenza at Yale University has recently used functional magnetic resonance imaging (MRI) to compare the brain regions involved in drug cravings in cocaine users with those involved in gambling cravings in pathological gamblers. Evidence from this study suggests that the same mesocorticolimbic dopamine circuitry (that is, the reward circuit) and the front part of the brain may be involved in both drug-related and non–drug-related urges.

Imaging studies in other impulse control disorders have not been performed. Given our current lack of knowledge of the other impulse control disorders, however, imaging studies may be premature at this point.

One final line of evidence that may provide clues to the mechanism involved in impulse control disorders is treatment response. Although a cause cannot be inferred from a response to medication, the fact that people respond to serotonin reuptake inhibitors and to opioid antagonists suggests that disturbed brain chemistry plays an important role in either causing or perpetuating these disorders. After being treated, Ken characterized his pathological gambling as a disorder of brain chemistry: "I stopped having urges to gamble once I started taking medication. It was like a miracle. Before I took medication, I just assumed there was something wrong with my willpower. My response made me believe that this was really an illness in my brain." Various treatments and response rates will be discussed in a later chapter.

Genetic studies may be yet another means of determining the neurobiological basis for impulse control disorders. One study of twins by Wendy Slutske at the University of Missouri has found that pathological gambling is more common in the twin of someone suffering from pathological gambling than in the twins of control subjects. The fact that monozygotic twins appear to have higher rates of pathological gambling than dizygotic twins suggests a genetic cause. The study also found shared genetic vulnerability between pathological gambling and alcohol dependence. Although the study of possible genetic causes of impulse control disorders is just beginning, these findings should come as no surprise. In fact, most psychiatric disorders appear to be caused by a combination of neurobiological, environmental, and genetic factors. The neurobiological bases of impulse control disorders are most probably genetically transmitted. Although no genetic studies have been done on the other impulse control disorders, we consistently see elevated rates of impulse control disorders in the family members of people we treat for all the impulse control disorders. "My mother suffered from compulsive shopping, and so do I," Amy began. "Even my younger sister is starting to show symptoms of the disorder—she misses family events to go to the mall, and she's acquiring a lot of credit card debt. I believe this problem runs in my family, that there's something wrong with our genes." Although learned behavior may be an important contributor in cases such as this, genetics may also have a role.

As a whole, the studies of impulse control disorders provide many clues to the neurochemical and neuroanatomic systems involved in these disorders. Nevertheless, a great deal remains to be learned. Further studies to determine the neurobiological commonalities among the impulse control disorders should be undertaken. An understanding of the neurobiology of impulse control disorders may be of value in treating not only these disorders, but also similar disorders such as alcoholism and other drug addictions.

Psychological Perspectives on Impulse Control Disorders

Hal, who suffered from pathological gambling, described his disorder in psychological terms. "I think my gambling is a way for me to rebel. I always do the right thing—I'm always so responsible, always helping others. Gambling, I think, is my way to act like a bad boy— and it's thrilling, in part, because I shouldn't be doing it." For some people, are impulse control disorders an expression of underlying psychological issues? Do early interactions within the family put one at risk for developing an impulse control disorder? What about the role of personality or temperament?

Psychological explanations for impulse control disorders have a long history.

For example, Freud described gambling as a need for self-punishment, as a means of coping with and ridding oneself of guilt, and as a reflection of men's ambivalence toward their fathers. Others, building upon this concept of the gambler as masochist, saw gambling as a rebellion against the authority of the parents and the reality principle that they represent. Some people describe the onset of their impulse control behavior in terms of their psychological relationship with their parents. One man talked about his compulsive sexual behavior in similar terms: "I sometimes wonder if I started having a lot of sex because my parents were so religious. In my gut I knew it would've killed them if they had known. And although I was always ashamed of myself, I still couldn't stop."

Some researchers have turned to causes rooted in childhood experiences in order to understand gambling and other impulse disorders. Theories of parental deprivation have been described, with the compulsive person turning to games of chance, shopping, or sex for the attention and emotional response that has been denied them. The theory is that when parental stimulation has been lacking, people turn to activities that increase stimulation.

Some researchers have suggested that impulse control disorders arise from the unconscious displacement of sexual conflict. Performing "forbidden acts" in a "secret" fashion (that is, not telling others about the behavior) has been likened to a sexual act. The theory suggests that such a person's real sexual life is underdeveloped and that the addictive behavior is a substitute for sexual arousal.

Still others have described behavioral addictions as attempts to ward off depressive feelings. The risk-taking behavior that we see in impulse control disorders may have antidepressant effects. In fact, people who engage in impulsive behavior often describe depressive states. Approximately 40 to 50 percent of the people we treat report a current or prior episode of depression. Stephanie described the way she felt when she engaged in compulsive sexual behavior: "I didn't think about sex except when I got depressed. I think the sex was a way of coping with feeling sad and lonely. It seemed to relieve my depression. Maybe it was the thrill of doing something bad."

The psychological explanation that impulse control behavior is related to feelings of depression again highlights the intimate connection between the neurobiological and the psychological. It has been suggested that people with impulse control disorders engage in risk-taking behavior as a means of stimulating the opioid system. The opioid release "soothes" the person; it treats his or her sadness or reduces his or her anxiety. Thus, impulsive behavior is a mechanism for relieving a chronic state of hyperarousal, perhaps produced by prior stressful or traumatic events, and thereby managing depression or anxiety. "When I feel stressed or depressed, I steal," one woman told me. "I find it so comforting. Later, I regret having done it. But at the time, it really gets me through some tough situations."

Psychological theories such as these are difficult to prove or disprove. In our view, these theories alone do not provide a satisfactory explanation of why people develop impulse control disorders. Many people with impulse control disorders do not report any underlying psychological conflicts. Also, the fact that people respond well to treatment with medications and cognitive behavior therapy would suggest that underlying psychological conflicts are not the primary explanation for these disorders. In our experience, dynamic psychotherapy and psychoanalysis, although useful for other psychological difficulties, have not provided relief from the symptoms of impulse control disorders.

Although these various psychological factors may not be the cause of impulse control disorders, they may be considered risk factors for the development of these disorders. What psychological factors might contribute to impulse control disorders? One possible factor might be peer interactions during adolescence. Take shopping, for example. Although shopping usually starts with one's parents, shopping with peers is often the first time a person controls his or her money and makes independent decisions about purchases. Many of our patients report that their first exposure to gambling, sex, or stealing came about through interactions with their peers. Peers may also place an emphasis on such behavior. David, a twenty-six-year-old man, told me, "I started to gamble in high school because my friends did. I wanted to fit in, so I would play cards too." One woman described adolescence as the beginning of her illness: "I think the shopping became a problem when my friends would insist on going to the mall all the time. They made me believe that I had to wear something new to school each day if I wanted to be popular. I wanted them to like me." Cynthia, now thirty-seven years old, stole clothing with her friends during adolescence. "They would dare me to do it. They did it too. The problem was that I couldn't stop."

Although some researchers have suggested that problematic family situations during adolescence may contribute to impulse control disorders, there is very little systematic data pertaining to family experiences in people with these disorders. Although the exact role of parenting behavior in the development of impulse control disorders is unknown, we have researched perceptions of parental care and protection in people with pathological gambling and kleptomania. We found that people with these disorders often describe their parents as both less caring and less protective than people without psychiatric illnesses generally do. These findings are consistent with the way these people describe their early life experiences, often emphasizing the emotional neglect of their parents.

One other area of family research has focused on the relatives of people with impulse control disorders. Our research has generally found elevated rates of alcohol use problems in first-degree relatives of people with impulse control disorders, often as high as 30 to 60 percent. This high rate of alcohol abuse in first-degree relatives of our patients is also consistent with studies of alcoholic families. Relatively high levels of behavioral disinhibition differentiate the children of alcoholics from those of nonalcoholics. Just as general behavioral disinhibition may be familial, the development of impulse control disorders may be similarly affected by this behavioral trait. This finding is another example of the overlap between psychological and neurobiological theories; however, the exact influence of genetics and environmental risk factors is just beginning to be explored.

Are there certain personality traits that may predispose a person to the development of an impulse control disorder? Personality may be another area that crosses the boundary between the psychological and the neurobiological, as personality traits may be both environmental and genetic. Also, personality traits may not be the same for all impulse control disorders.

For example, people with pathological gambling tend to seek novel experiences and exhibit general impulsiveness. They also tend to be socially avoidant and to have slightly higher scores on "neuroticism," a measure of anxiety, depression, self-consciousness, and feelings of vulnerability, than people with no psychiatric illnesses. People with kleptomania appear to share many of the same personality traits. They are also generally impulsive and score high on scales of novelty-seeking and neuroticism. The one difference is that people with kleptomania also tend to be insensitive, practical, and tough-minded, which are traits not generally found among pathological gamblers. These latter traits, however, may simply reflect the fact that people with kleptomania have fewer social attachments, most likely because of the intense guilt and shame that their illegal behavior causes them. Neither people with pathological gambling nor those with kleptomania appear to have severe obsessional traits. There are not enough data regarding the personality traits of compulsive shoppers or people with compulsive sexual behavior to make meaningful comments. However, based on our clinical experience, they too appear to share many of the personality traits seen in people with pathological gambling and kleptomania.

Some researchers have argued that people with impulse control disorders may have a lack of regard for rules and laws. In our clinical work with people with impulse control disorders, we do not generally see the personality trait of psychopathy, or the disregard for the rights and welfare of others. Neither do we see many people with impulse control disorders who also suffer from antisocial personality disorder, a more pervasive pattern of behavior that causes people to violate social norms.

Although people with impulse control disorders appear to have certain distinct personality traits, what is the relationship of these traits to the actual illnesses? Do certain personality traits cause impulse control disorders, or do the disorders lead to the development of distinct personality traits? Because both impulse control disorders and personality traits usually have their onset in adolescence, it is difficult to say which comes first.

Psychological factors in impulse control disorders need to be better understood. Do these psychological factors determine what type of impulse control disorder someone may develop? Do they determine, for example, what the person with kleptomania steals or what the person with compulsive shopping purchases? It seems clear that certain psychological factors influence the presentation of these disorders and may also represent risk factors for their development. It is likely, however, that these psychological factors act in concert with the neurobiological elements to ultimately form the illnesses we know as impulse control disorders.

The Role of Society in Impulse Control Disorders

Although social and cultural messages do not appear to actually cause impulse control disorders, they may trigger the urges and the behaviors. One man told me, "I only think about stealing things when I see items on television that look attractive. That causes the urges to steal." Another woman reported, "When I hear radio advertisements telling me about 'winning big' and all that I could do with extra money, that's when I have urges to gamble. Otherwise I don't think about gambling much." And finally, a woman who suffered from compulsive shopping described her disorder in these terms: "I watch soap operas all day. The homes always look so beautiful. Fancy appliances, wonderful-looking furniture. That's when I have cravings to shop. I know I can't afford those things, but I want them so badly after seeing them on television. One week when our television wasn't working, I didn't shop at all. I thought I was cured, but then we got a new television and I was back at it."

Three of the disorders we have been discussing involve consumerism—that is, acquiring money or possessions is the reward. Pathological gambling is about winning money. Kleptomania is about getting something for nothing, possessing items. Compulsive shopping also concerns the acquisition of things. How do these disorders relate to messages seen on television, in films, or in magazines? Isn't everyone in our society concerned with acquiring money or possessions? Isn't the acquisition of money and possessions the goal advanced by advertising and our consumer culture?

The idea that we should accumulate items or money is everywhere: on television, in magazines, and in films. The acquisition of possessions or money is often glamorized, even if the means by which one acquires these items is illegal. Contemporary culture presents gambling as attractive. Winning large amounts of money at a casino is characterized as the answer to life's problems. Similarly, shopping, even to excess, is portrayed in glamorous ways. Credit card debt is often trivialized with a "live for the moment" attitude. Even stealing is often portrayed in television and movies as carefree, adolescent fun. In fact, the message of consumer culture is often that people should want things or money, and should acquire them at any cost.

Is it possible that society's focus on the acquisition of possessions and money contributes to the occurrence of these impulse control disorders? Many of the people we treat for pathological gambling report that casino advertisements suggesting the possibility of winning large amounts of money increase their symptoms. People with compulsive shopping often tell us that the media's and society's message that buying things results in happiness increases the frequency of their behavior. Even people with kleptomania, who may never steal items that they want, describe their stealing behavior as exacerbated by the constant portrayal of the thrill associated with getting something for nothing.

The role of sociocultural influences in compulsive sexual behavior is somewhat different. The common element in this illness is society's insistence on eroticism. People with compulsive sexual behavior have told us that their compulsive behavior worsens when they are constantly bombarded by attractive people on television, in films, or in magazines who are marketed in sexually suggestive ways (for example, wearing either revealing or very little clothing). "Sometimes I go for days without urges for promiscuous sex," Jeff told me. "Then I start watching some television show with women in swimsuits, and I get so revved up. I then start the whole ordeal of spending a lot of time looking for and having sex. It's like the television show has set off this big snowball. Don't misunderstand me. I have these urges even when I don't see things on television, but certain television shows can make it a lot worse. I have to be very careful about what I watch."

These disorders have been described for centuries, so modern advertising and other social influences are obviously not the cause of these illnesses. Virtually none of the people we treat believe that these social or cultural influences are the cause of their disorder. But they often point to these influences as worsening their urges or their behavior. If there is a genetic vulnerability to these disorders, it may be possible that these sociocultural influences increase a person's risk of developing an impulse control disorder, or possibly worsen a disorder once a person has it. Does this mean that as we are exposed to more social influences that place a priority on money, possessions, and sex, we will see an increase in the prevalence of these disorders? The answer to this question is unknown. Further research is needed to shed light on the factors influencing these disorders.

Willpower, Morals, and Character

Willpower, morals, and character are three factors that have no causal relationship to impulse control disorders. We mention them because people often feel that a lack of one of these factors is the reason they suffer from these disorders. As we stated earlier, shame and secrecy are seemingly intrinsic to these disorders. People who feel that their impulse control disorder is due to their lack of willpower, or to moral or character flaws, suffer intense guilt and are less likely to seek treatment for their illnesses.

Doris, a fifty-three-year-old married woman, introduced herself by saying, "I'm a horrible person. Who does this sort of thing?" Doris had suffered from kleptomania for over thirty years. "I break one of the Ten Commandments every week. Only an evil person could continue to do that. I can't even go to church any longer because I know what kind of person I am. God wants nothing to do with me."

John, a twenty-three-year-old man who suffered from pathological gambling, described himself in these terms: "I don't want to gamble, and yet I keep going to the casinos. I must be a really weak person if I can't stop myself from gambling. If I had more willpower, I could stop. I must not want to get better."

"I think it's all about character," Wendy said when describing her compulsive shopping. "I must shop a lot because my character is flawed. Anyone worth admiring wouldn't have this problem. It's a weakness in my character."

People do not develop impulse control disorders because of a general lack of willpower, moral weakness, or weakness of character. Although there are no studies of the morality or character strength of people with these disorders, in our clinical experience, these people are as moral as any other person and have characters that are as stable and admirable as anyone else's. In fact, the extreme guilt many of these people suffer attests to their moral character. People with impulse control disorders often try to assert their willpower and not engage in certain behaviors. The problem is that the urges to engage in these behaviors are often overwhelming— that is the definition of these illnesses. With proper treatment, the urges are reduced enough that a person can more easily resist them.

Impulse control disorders are psychiatric illnesses. These disorders most probably have definite neurobiological causes, to which psychological and environmental factors contribute. Thus, trying hard to change is rarely an adequate solution to these very disabling illnesses. We hope that by making it known that the cause of these disorders is biological, we will encourage those who suffer from these illnesses to seek treatment. As we discuss in a later chapter, there are effective treatments that address the underlying biological roots of these illnesses.

8

Medication Treatment for Impulse Control Disorders

Janice, a fifty-five-year-old woman, suffered from kleptomania. She stole clothing from a local department store approximately two or three times each week. "I have these cravings to steal when I wake up in the morning. I try to avoid shopping so that I won't be in a position to steal, but when the urges are strong, I go right to the store after breakfast." Janice's urges to steal were often triggered by her mood. "When I feel lonely or depressed, the cravings are so much worse. I work in sales, and when I go home, I don't have much to keep me busy. So I think about what I'm lacking—a husband and children. Those thoughts get me down. It's usually the morning after a night of crying that I have the urges." Janice was initially treated with naltrexone for her stealing urges. Approximately four days after reaching a dose of 150 mg/day of naltrexone, Janice reported that her urges were essentially gone.

At a follow-up appointment, Janice expressed her happiness with the improvement, but also her difficulties: "The problem is that

I continue to steal. I don't really have cravings to do so any longer, but it feels more like a habit after all these years. I've been stealing for at least twenty-five years. Who am I if I stop?" Janice was then started on an antidepressant (a selective serotonin reuptake inhibitor [SSRI]) and began therapy. As her overall mood improved, Janice stopped stealing completely. Therapy assisted her in making the transition into a life without stealing and into an identity that was not based on her behavior. Janice, who had not gone a week without stealing for the previous twenty-five years, has now been without symptoms of kleptomania for more than a year.

Clark, a thirty-eight-year-old business executive, came to our clinic for treatment of his gambling addiction. Clark gambled approximately four nights each week. On an average evening, he might lose as much as $2000. He would spend hours at the casino playing blackjack, often not going home until the next morning. Thoughts of gambling preoccupied him, and these thoughts kept him from working as effectively as he had in the past. "I only started gambling about three years ago. I think it became a problem almost immediately. I can't point to any definite triggers to why I gamble. I know I love the thrill of winning, and occasionally I do win. I think that's what keeps me going back." Clark did not suffer from any other psychiatric problems. Clark agreed to a trial of an SSRI, citalopram. After reaching a dose of 60 mg/day, Clark returned to the clinic. "I haven't been gambling for the past couple of weeks. I can't believe it, but I'm not even thinking about gambling. I just don't have any drive to go to the casino. I'm pretty happy just staying home at night."

"I probably buy something at least three times a week," Amy said as she described her illness. "I don't think I want half of the stuff I purchase, but buying it seems to make me feel good. I work as a legal secretary, and recently I have been leaving the office early to go to the stores. It doesn't really matter, I guess, because all I think about at work is the next thing I'm going to buy. Why am I so obsessed with shopping? I never used to be. Only during the last year has this become such a problem." Amy agreed to a trial of an antidepressant, the SSRI paroxetine. After several weeks on a maximum dose of 60 mg/day, Amy reported that her shopping was much more under control. "I'm a lot better at not going to the stores. I seem to have more power to stop myself. I'm feeling a lot better about myself now that I have more control over this illness." However, Amy was still obsessing about shopping approximately six to eight hours each day, a significant amount of time, and this was interfering with her life. Amy then added an atypical neuroleptic medication, olanzapine, to her paroxetine. Even taking a relatively low dose of 5 mg/day, Amy reported that her obsessions with shopping had disappeared. "I feel that these medications have been miracles. I have my life back. And I don't have to worry about losing my job."

Impulse control disorders typically present many challenges to effective treatment. Until recently, psychiatrists rarely paid attention to the question of whether medications might help decrease the urges and behaviors associated with impulse control disorders. Now, however, there are several promising developments in the use of medications for these disorders. We will discuss the different medications that have been used to treat these disorders, describe the pros and cons of each medication, and provide guidelines as to which medications are most promising for various presentations of these illnesses.

"I Didn't Know This Problem Could Be Treated with Medication": Barriers to Treatment

One woman told us, "I have been talking to my primary physician for years about my gambling problem, and he never recommended any medication for it. He told me to see a psychiatrist. I put it off for years because I didn't think I was crazy. When I finally became really depressed by all of the financial problems the gambling has caused, I went to see a psychiatrist. I told her all about my gambling addiction. She didn't mention anything about medication to me."

For many people with impulse control disorders, locating a professional with the necessary experience to help them can be a difficult task. Because so little had been written on these disorders until recently, many psychiatrists and family physicians still lack information about these illnesses and are unfamiliar with the available treatments. In fact, many psychiatrists continue to see impulse control disorders as a form of obsessive-compulsive disorder, even though these disorders and their treatments appear to be different in many ways. (Please see Appendix A for referral sources.)

Although finding a mental health professional with experience in impulse control disorders is necessary for effective treatment, this is not the only barrier that presents itself. Helen, a woman suffering from compulsive shopping, was brought to our clinic by her husband. "She doesn't think she has a problem," Helen's husband began. "We are one step away from bankruptcy because of her constant shopping, and yet she refuses to get help." Helen worked in marketing and was an educated woman. Apparently her shopping had gotten out of control about two years prior to this appointment. The shopping had worsened in frequency over the last two years. "I just don't believe this is an illness," Helen interjected. "I think I should be able to stop on my own. Who goes to see a psychiatrist because they shop too much? Just because I shop a lot doesn't mean I'm crazy." Helen eventually agreed to be started on a medication, but she failed to return for follow-up appointments. When I called her to find out why she was canceling appointments, Helen told me, "I'm sorry, but I can't come back. I just don't think this is an illness or that I need a doctor for it."

One obvious barrier to treatment, even when a competent mental health professional can be found, is the person's inability to acknowledge that he or she has an illness and that he or she needs professional psychiatric help. However, most people are able to recognize that they have a problem if they assess the amount of time lost to the urges and impulsive behavior, the emotional distress the disorder produces, and the extent to which the urges, thoughts, or behavior associated with the disorder interfere with their lives.

Even when a person recognizes the problem, that is no guarantee that he or she will seek professional psychiatric help. Instead, many people attempt to control the problem on their own. For example, the compulsive shopper and the person with kleptomania may refuse to go to stores, the pathological gambler may distract himself by starting new projects at home, and the person with compulsive sexual behavior may decrease the amount of time she spends away from her spouse or family as a means of reducing temptation. For many people, it is necessary first to acknowledge to themselves either that these approaches do not work or that they cause an equally severe, but different, form of emotional distress. Once they have done so, they are more willing to seek professional assistance.

Even once they are willing to seek help, however, people with impulse control disorders must be aware that the problem they are suffering from is an illness that psychiatrists treat. One man told me, "At first I didn't even know that my stealing had a name. I had never heard of kleptomania. I also didn't have any idea that doctors could treat this. I thought I should just go see my priest." A woman described her attempts to get help for her kleptomania: "My primary physician told me to just quit stealing. I tried so hard to stop myself, but I couldn't. I knew he'd be angry or disappointed, so I quit seeing him or any other doctor. When I found out that my stealing was an actual psychiatric illness, I was so relieved. When I found out that there were medications that might help me stop, I cried. I had lived with this problem for so long, thinking it was my fault and thinking no one could ever help me."

A final barrier to effective treatment is often a person's reluctance to stop these behaviors. Gaining compliance with medication treatment in impulse control disorders faces challenges similar to those in certain other psychiatric illnesses, such as bipolar disorder and substance dependence. People suffering from mania may not comply with treatment with mood stabilizers in part because drug treatment may reduce the positive or euphoric experiences associated with hypomania or mania. Similarly, with substance use disorders, there is a pleasurable component to drug use that often makes people ambivalent regarding taking medications to help them stop using drugs, or to become or remain abstinent in general.

In the case of impulse control disorders, gambling, shopping, stealing, and sex are often pleasurable even when they cause a person significant problems. Therefore, even when there are treatments available, and even when a person suffering from one of these disorders finds a physician who is knowledgeable about these problems, the person may be ambivalent about treatment because of some sense of pleasure or relief associated with the behaviors. Public education about impulse control disorders, and about the difficulties they cause, is necessary to enable people to overcome these barriers and receive effective treatment.

Medications Useful for Impulse Control Disorders

Only a few controlled studies of the use of medications to treat impulse control disorders have been done, but the results appear promising. Thus far, the use of serotonin reuptake inhibitors (either clomipramine or SSRIs), the opioid antagonist naltrexone, mood stabilizers, and atypical neuroleptics has met with varying degrees of success. Additional strategies targeting urge and behavior reduction and mechanisms for coping with urges and behavior (e.g., cognitive behavior therapies) may represent important adjunctive components.

Because the Food and Drug Administration (FDA) currently has yet to approve any medications for treating impulse control disorders, people should be aware that this is an "off-label" use, as well as recognize the empirical basis for considering treatment with medications. People should also realize that available evidence about treatment is limited and that there is still much that we do not know about how to treat these disorders.

The first class of medication that we will discuss as showing benefit for people with impulse control disorders is serotonin reuptake inhibitors (SRIs). SRIs are antidepressant medications with antiobsessional properties. In addition to being effective in treating depression and obsessive-compulsive disorder, SRIs are also used to treat eating disorders, panic disorder, and social phobia. It is primarily psychiatrists that prescribe these medications, although many family physicians have experience with them. The SRIs currently available in the United States are clomipramine (Anafranil), citalopram (Celexa), fluoxetine (Prozac), fluvoxamine (Luvox), paroxetine (Paxil), and sertraline (Zoloft). The last five medications are often referred to as selective SRIs because, unlike clomipramine, they affect serotonin more than they affect other chemicals in the brain.

Response to SRIs usually involves a decrease in thoughts about the impulsive behavior, a decrease in impulsive behavior, and improvement in social and occupational functioning. Patients may initially report feeling less preoccupied with the behavior and feeling less anxious about having thoughts of the behavior. For people who engage in impulsive behavior because their urges are linked with their mood, SRIs are a reasonable first-line medication.

As in the treatment of obsessive-compulsive disorder, the doses of SRIs required to treat impulse control symptoms appear to be higher than the average doses generally required to treat depressive disorders. Some studies have suggested that there is a significant initial response in people with impulse control disorders that may be largely a result of the placebo effect. That is, some people appear to improve regardless of the dose or the medication. This response may be due to having talked about their problem for the first time or to feeling that they are being supported in their illness. This placebo response means that improvement should be monitored for several months and that patients and clinicians need to be cautious about early improvement. An SRI should not be considered ineffective unless it has been tried for at least ten to twelve weeks and the highest dose tolerated by the patient or recommended by the manufacturer has been reached.

Is there one SRI that is the best for a particular impulse control disorder? This question has not been examined in a systematic fashion. However, people suffering from impulse control disorders may respond to one medication and not to another. Therefore, if the first medication is not effective in reducing symptoms of the impulse control disorder, a second, and even a third, medication should be tried.

Lauren, a twenty-seven-year-old woman, sought help for compulsive shopping because of the financial problems it was causing and the toll it was taking on her marriage. "There must be something wrong with me. I have a great husband, and yet I can't stop doing the one thing that is driving him away. I'm obsessed with buying things, usually just stupid things I don't need. When I get obsessed with it, I don't seem to care about anything else, including my husband. I'm so frustrated, and pretty hopeless that anything will help me. I'm in too deep." Lauren was started on citalopram, and after several weeks, she reported little or no change in her symptoms. Although she was even more frustrated with her illness at this point, Lauren agreed to be patient and try another medication. She was then switched to fluvoxamine, and after four weeks she reported that her obsessive thoughts of shopping were significantly improved.

Another woman we were treating for compulsive sexual behavior was initially tried on fluoxetine. She suffered from severe obsessionality concerning her sexual behavior, thinking about sex an average of eight hours every day. She engaged in sex to the point of losing her marriage and custody of her children. The thoughts of sex significantly interfered with her ability to work. After several weeks and several dose adjustments, she reported that she was too frustrated with her lack of improvement to continue taking the fluoxetine. She continued to have sex compulsively and feared she would lose her job as a result of her inability to complete projects. She was then switched to fluvoxamine, and again reported no improvement after several weeks. She was then reminded that often several medications need to be tried. After several weeks on citalopram, she reported that her thoughts of sex and her sexual behavior were significantly reduced. She was better able to function at work and was able to complete several overdue projects.

Another class of medication that has been effective in treating impulse control disorders is opioid antagonists. Naltrexone appears to be a reasonable first-line agent for patients who report intense urges to engage in impulsive behavior. Many patients who report "obsessions" with these behaviors may actually be suffering from uncontrollable urges that interfere with daily functioning. When the urges are eliminated or reduced, the preoccupation often disappears. People taking naltrexone often report less intense urges. The urges may not go away completely, but they are often reduced enough to enable the patient to resist them. Patients also report enjoying the particular impulsive behavior less when they are taking naltrexone: The "high" associated with the behavior is reduced.

Naltrexone has been tested in various psychiatric conditions in which urges are a dominant symptom. The use of naltrexone in the treatment of alcohol dependence and opiate dependence has the greatest amount of evidence supporting it, and both of these uses are FDA-approved indications.

In the case of impulse control disorders, there is a small body of literature suggesting that naltrexone is effective. Case reports describe people suffering from compulsive sexual behavior who have responded to naltrexone. Our first study using naltrexone in pathological gambling showed a significant decline in the intensity of urges to gamble, gambling thoughts, and gambling behavior when using, on average, 150 mg/day. This was followed by a larger study in which an average naltrexone dose of 150 to 200 mg/day resulted in an improvement in gambling urges, thoughts, and behavior. Similarly, we conducted the first medication study on kleptomania and found naltrexone to be effective in reducing stealing urges and behavior, again at a dose of approximately 150 mg/day. Although there are no studies using naltrexone to treat compulsive shopping, we find it clinically useful in people who have urges to shop.

Erin, a forty-three-year-old woman, reported intense urges to buy things. After several months of symptoms, she was unable to run her dry cleaning business because of her almost constant preoccupation with purchasing items. Depressed and with severe financial difficulties, Erin sought treatment in our clinic. "If I don't stop this behavior, I'll lose my business. That business means everything to me. I don't think I could go on living without it. I'm feeling pretty desperate." Erin was initially started on an SSRI, paroxetine. With gradual dose increases, Erin reported an improvement in her mood. She no longer felt as hopeless as she had when she initially presented, and she was better able to cope with the financial stress of her business, but she was still shopping. "Maybe it's a little less. I guess the intensity of my thoughts and urges has decreased, but those urges are still there. I still can't resist them most of the time. I am better on the medication, but I still have little control over my shopping."

Erin was then started on naltrexone along with her paroxetine. After informing her about the possible dangers of using over-the-counter analgesics like aspirin or Tylenol with naltrexone, we started her at 25 mg/day. Although Erin reported some mild nausea at first, it went away after about the third day on the medication. Her dose of naltrexone was gradually increased to 100 mg/day. After taking that dose for two weeks, Erin returned to the clinic. "The urges are gone. I don't know what you did, but I'm not shopping. I have no desire to shop. It's like I'm finally free of this problem. This medication saved my life." Erin has not shown symptoms of compulsive shopping for over a year.

A third class of medication, mood stabilizers, has also gained increasing clinical attention in the treatment of impulsive behaviors. Mood stabilizers are anticonvulsant medications (i.e., medications used to treat seizures) that have been shown to be effective in treating bipolar disorder (manic-depressive illness). These medications are also often used to treat migraines and pain caused by nerve problems. In the case of impulse control disorders, people suffering from pathological gambling have reported successful responses to lithium and carbamazepine (Tegretol). Preliminary evidence concerning the use of divalproex (Depakote) in the treatment of pathological gambling and kleptomania further supports the notion that mood stabilizers may be useful for impulse control disorders. The benefit from carbamazepine, lithium, and divalproex may be due to the efficacy of these drugs in the treatment of bipolar disorder and the existence of features shared by impulse control disorders and bipolar disorder (e.g., impulsivity).

"I can't take it anymore. The courts told me that if I were caught stealing one more time, I'd have to go to jail for at least ninety days. I was terrified, and yet I left the courthouse and within thirty minutes was taking something from a jewelry store. What kind of person does that?" Samantha was tearful as she described her almost constant urges to steal. "I don't know if you can understand what this is like. It's like there's something inside of me that I hate and I can't control. I'll kill myself before I go to jail. Maybe I should just kill myself anyway and get it over with." Samantha suffered from kleptomania and depression, and after this initial interview in our clinic needed to be hospitalized. She was started on an antidepressant in the hospital, and after several weeks her mood had improved significantly. However, she continued to steal. "I feel better, but my behavior's no different. I was hoping I'd stop once I started to feel more like my old self, but now I'm not sure I'll ever stop this." After discussion of several medication options, Samantha agreed to a trial of valproic acid. After three weeks and achieving a dose of 1500 mg/day, she returned to the clinic. "I haven't stolen anything in about the last seven to ten days. I'm not sure why. I can't believe it's the medication. It must be something else. No pill could stop what I've been doing, could it?" Although she reports occasional thoughts about stealing and urges to steal, Samantha has not stolen anything for almost a year.

The final class of medications worth exploring in the treatment of impulse control disorders is atypical neuroleptics. Although there is little evidence that atypical antipsychotics are useful in impulse control disorders when used alone, augmentation of SSRIs with clinically atypical neuroleptics (that is, adding these medications to an SSRI to enhance its effectiveness) may be beneficial. The following medications are atypical neuroleptics: olanzapine (Zyprexa), quetiapine (Seroquel), risperidone (Risperdal), ziprasidone (Geodon), and clozapine (Clozaril). Because they block the chemical dopamine in the brain, atypical neuroleptics were initially used to treat delusional or psychotic disorders. The use of atypical antipsychotics as augmenting agents in the treatment of nonpsychotic disorders and behaviors, including obsessive-compulsive disorder, has also been explored. Although there are no studies examining the use of these medications in impulse control disorders, clinically we find that adding these medications to an SSRI is often quite effective in reducing the thoughts and urges associated with the impulse control disorder.

"I've been gambling for the past six years," Matthew began. "I can't really say that it's caused severe work problems for me, but I have probably lost every relationship I had. My friends got so tired of me borrowing money and not paying it back. My wife accused me of loving the casino more than her—and she was probably right. So she left me a year ago. I've been to groups and nothing seems to work." Matthew told his gambling story without emotion in his voice and without changing his facial expression. Because he used narcotic pain medications daily as a result of a severe back injury, Matthew was not a candidate for naltrexone. Instead, he was started on an SSRI. After reaching a maximum dose and continuing on it for three months, Matthew told me that he felt better, that his thoughts of gambling were much less frequent. The problem was that the thoughts had not disappeared. He still had symptoms, and he still gambled, although less than before. Matthew and I discussed treatment options. I told him that because he had improved on the first medication, it made sense to keep him on it and simply add another medication. We discussed atypical neuroleptics and their possible side effects. Matthew was started on risperidone 1 mg/day, increasing to 2 mg/day. Matthew then reported even more improvement in his gambling obsession. The thoughts of gambling had disappeared almost entirely. Matthew stopped going to the casino. After several months without gambling, he was able to reconnect with some old friends, and he had even started talking to his wife about a possible reconciliation.

Other medications are just starting to be explored as possible treatments for impulse control disorders. For example, other types of antidepressants may also be useful in treating people with impulse control disorders. As we discuss later, antidepressants may be particularly useful in those people who engage in impulsive behavior because they feel sad, lonely, or depressed. Other possible antidepressant agents might include bupropion (Wellbutrin), nefazodone (Serzone), and venlafaxine (Effexor).

In addition to antidepressants, other classes of medication may also be useful. In particular, stimulants may help reduce impulsive behavior. Some researchers have suggested that impulse control disorders may be related to attention deficit hyperactivity disorder (ADHD). Because stimulants such as methylphenidate (Ritalin) are effective in treating ADHD, they may also have a role in treating impulsive behavior. Studies on these medications have yet to be done, but they may be promising options in the treatment of these disorders.

One final word should be said about herbal medicines and nutritional therapies. There is currently no sound scientific evidence that these treatments are effective for impulse control disorders. The use of untested therapies often wastes time and money. People who are taking these treatments should, however, inform their physicians, as they might interact in a negative, or possibly even life-threatening, way with other medications. Although many herbal medicines may offer potential hope for people with impulse control disorders, at the present time, with the currently available scientific evidence, we are somewhat skeptical of the efficacy of these alternative therapies in treating impulse control disorders.

Treatment: Response, Duration, and Side Effects

The degree of improvement with medication depends to some degree on the class of medication used and on the person being treated. SRIs are generally quite effective in the treatment of impulse control disorders. We estimate that approximately two-thirds of people treated with these agents will report some improvement in their symptoms. Most people will report that they spend less time preoccupied with thoughts of their behavior and that the thoughts are less tormenting. They may also find it easier to resist their thoughts, and this results in many people reporting that they feel they have better control over their thinking. In addition, people taking SRIs may report some decrease in their urges to engage in the impulsive behavior. Although improvement on SRIs appears to be independent of underlying depressive symptoms, treatment with these medications does improve mood and lessen the emotional pain that people with impulse control disorders often feel.

It often takes an average of ten to twelve weeks for symptoms of impulse control disorders to decrease by a significant amount with SRI treatment. Some people, of course, will respond as early as two weeks after beginning treatment, but this is the exception. Improvement tends to be quite gradual, with continued improvement often taking place over several months. A reduction in symptoms is more common than complete remission of symptoms. That is, it is more common for people to report a lessening of the impulsive thoughts or urges than to tell us that these thoughts or urges are completely gone.

There are currently no guidelines for the length of treatment trials for impulse control disorders. Available data suggest that adequate treatment of these disorders often requires a relatively long duration of treatment. In fact, a sustained drug treatment for impulse control disorders might require up to three months. Clinicians must monitor symptom response over a long enough period to assess the difference between the placebo effect (i.e., some people feel better after taking a pill, even if the pill is a sugar pill and has no active medication) and a response to medication.

What dose is necessary for improvement? Doses of SRIs similar to those typically used for obsessive-compulsive disorder and higher than those typically needed for major depression appear to be necessary for impulse control disorders. Maximum recommended doses of the SRIs are as follows: citalopram (Celexa), 60 mg/day; clomipramine (Anafranil), 250 mg/day; fluoxetine (Prozac), 80 mg/day; fluvoxamine (Luvox), 300 mg/day; paroxetine (Paxil), 60 mg/day; and sertraline (Zoloft), 200 mg/day. The authors' clinical experience suggests that an SRI should not be considered ineffective unless it has been tried for at least ten to twelve weeks and the highest dose tolerated by the patient or recommended by the manufacturer has been reached.

Because no one has yet conducted formal discontinuation studies and because there are very few data on the natural history of impulse control disorders, the optimal duration of treatment and rates of relapse associated with discontinuation of pharmacological treatment are presently not known. The authors' experiences suggest that many patients relapse upon discontinuation of pharmacological treatment and that long-term pharmacotherapy (e.g., for two or three years) may be warranted. However, the vast majority of our patients who respond to an SRI continue to do so over months or even years of taking the medication.

SRIs tend to be generally well tolerated, with usually only minimal side effects. The most common side effects include nausea, dry mouth, insomnia, feeling anxious, decreased sex drive or sexual functioning, and feeling tired. The medications are nonaddictive. Most side effects tend to be mild and tend to go away within the first couple of weeks of taking the medication.

Another class of medication that is useful in treating impulse control disorders is the opioid antagonists, of which naltrexone is the only currently marketed medication that has been used in treating these disorders. People taking naltrexone for impulse control disorders report that the medication decreases the urges or cravings to engage in the behavior or that they no longer feel the "high" or pleasure when engaging in the specific impulse behavior. High doses of naltrexone (150 to 200 mg/day) are usually necessary to reduce or eliminate the urges to engage in certain behaviors. Approximately 80 percent of people who suffer urges to engage in impulsive behaviors will see significant improvement when they take naltrexone.

In fact, about one-half of these people will report that their urges to engage in the behavior are completely eliminated. The other half of those who respond generally report that their urges are reduced enough that resisting them is much easier, and therefore that they are able to stop their impulsive behavior.

Clinically, a person will usually respond to a particular dose of naltrexone within two weeks. After that, an adjustment in dose is usually necessary. People often report nausea and diarrhea. Dizziness, sedation, and headaches occur less commonly. The side effects are usually mild and go away within the first week. Nausea, however, may be moderate to severe in some people. Therefore, we start people on 25 mg/day for the first three or four days to reduce the possibility of nausea. We may also give ondansetron 4 mg/day with the naltrexone for the same period to prevent the nausea.

Doses of naltrexone greater than 50 mg/day may, however, cause irritation of the liver. By taking blood samples, we monitor liver function closely in all people taking naltrexone. Of course, people with hepatitis, active liver disease, or liver failure should not take naltrexone. Initial liver function tests should be evaluated prior to starting naltrexone, and tests should be conducted again three to four weeks after starting the drug. Repeat testing should be performed at two- to four-week intervals for the next two months, a potential high-risk period. Thereafter, tests should be done approximately once a month for the following three months. After six months, irritation of the liver by naltrexone is quite rare, and testing three or four times a year should be sufficient unless people are putting their livers at risk in other ways, for example by excessive alcohol use. If the liver becomes irritated, naltrexone should be stopped. When this is done, the liver appears to return to normal.

Research in this area is still in an early stage, and practitioners prescribing the drug for impulse control disorders should be cautious when administering naltrexone at high doses and should monitor carefully for potential problems. Nonsteroidal analgesics (for example, aspirin, acetaminophen [Tylenol], ibuprofen [Motrin, Advil], etc.) should not be used in conjunction with high-dose naltrexone in the treatment of impulse control disorders. Their concurrent use seems to cause a higher risk of irritation of the liver.

The length of treatment with naltrexone is similar to that for treatment with SRIs. If people with impulse control disorders respond to a medication, they usually need to continue with that treatment for approximately two to three years before considering stopping the medication or the symptoms are likely to return.

More research on medications for impulse control disorders is seriously needed. Impulse control disorders appear to be chronic illnesses. People's symptoms do not generally spontaneously disappear for any extended period. The good news, however, is that there are medications for treating these disorders that are quite promising. More studies are required to better understand why certain people fail to respond to some or all of the possible treatments.

Treatment of Coexisting Psychiatric Disorders

It is not uncommon for people who suffer from impulse control disorders to also suffer from an additional coexisting psychiatric disorder. For example, people with pathological gambling often suffer from alcohol problems, depression, or anxiety. People with kleptomania may have a current mood disorder (depression or manic depression). Compulsive shoppers may also have problems with anxiety or mood disturbances. People with compulsive sexual behavior may also have difficulties with depression or substance abuse. And finally, a person may suffer from two or more impulse control disorders at the same time. The coexistence of other illnesses is important to recognize, as the treatment may have to be modified to account for them.

When one is attempting to understand comorbidity (the simultaneous existence of two or more illnesses), establishing the temporal relationship of the two disorders is intuitively appealing. Which disorder started first? Did one cause the other? If one is treated, will the other go away? Which one do we treat first? However, clearly establishing and interpreting such patterns of association has proved challenging. The simple case in which one of the disorders invariably precedes the other might suggest a direct causal relationship. Of course, there may be a third variable (for example, shared genes or a biological disturbance) that served as a common cause for both conditions. Further complicating the picture, causal associations may appear on a microbehavioral level (for example, alcohol use may disinhibit a person, resulting in a wide range of inappropriate behaviors, including problematic gambling) or on a macrodiagnostic level (for example, a person may develop pathological gambling as a substitute for drinking after treatment for alcoholism).

Regardless of the specific causal association linking impulse control disorders with these other illnesses, the fact that they frequently co-occur raises important treatment issues. Treatment of either the impulse control disorder or the other psychiatric illness could be complicated or even compromised by the presence of the other untreated condition. Treating one disorder alone will not be effective if the second disorder is exerting a causal or maintaining influence on the treated condition. Even in the more likely event that the impulse control disorder and the other disorder are associated via the influence of a third variable that can promote both disorders, treating one condition but not the other is potentially problematic. For example, the hopelessness associated with depression is likely to place a person at high risk for engaging in compulsive sexual behavior. Furthermore, the intensity of treatment needs to be addressed, as people with comorbid disorders are likely to have more functional impairment and a poorer prognosis than those with only a single condition.

Although clinically we believe that a person with several disorders needs treatment for all of these illnesses simultaneously, there is virtually no scientific literature on the temporal association of comorbid disorders with impulse control disorders and on the most effective treatment strategies for comorbidity in this group. For example, those with mood disorders in addition to the impulse control disorder may benefit from antidepressant treatment (a treatment currently recommended for impulse control disorders), and this may be particularly important when treating someone's impulse behavior with a medication such as naltrexone. Leaving a person's depression untreated would strongly predict a future relapse to the behavioral addiction. Similarly, a person with substance abuse may benefit from treatment for chemical dependency in addition to the treatment for impulsive behavior. Because impulse control disorders, like most psychiatric disorders, generally start in adolescence or early adulthood, it is important that treatment interventions capture individuals early when they are at risk for both disorders.

Another research area that has not yet been adequately developed would be an attempt to determine whether certain subtypes of people with impulse control disorders are more or less likely to have or develop a comorbid disorder. For example, there is some evidence indicating that strong subjective urges of the sort linked to specific brain regions are an important dynamic in the motivation to engage in certain behavior. That is, some disorder subtypes may be associated with neurobiological processes that overlap for both impulse control disorders and other psychiatric illnesses, whereas other subtypes of these disorders may have a different etiology that is unrelated to that of the comorbid condition. Research findings from genetic and brain-imaging studies will help to further identify key subgrouping variables and possible common biological substrates associated with both impulse control disorders and many of the comorbid disorders.

Guidelines for Medication Strategies

Despite the relatively early stage of investigations into what drug treatments for impulse control disorders are effective and well tolerated, it is important to consider whether distinct groups of individuals with impulse control disorders may respond better or worse to specific medications and whether distinct groups might represent treatment-refractory populations. In clinical settings, it is not unusual to encounter people who have had no response or only a partial response to treatment and thus require further treatment. We define treatment-refractory impulse control disorders as those in which people continue to experience significant symptoms following a trial of (1) an SRI at an adequate dose for an adequate duration (at least ten to twelve weeks) or (2) naltrexone at an adequate dose for an adequate duration (at least four to six weeks).

There is relatively little published data on pharmacological approaches to treatment-resistant impulse control disorders. In our clinical experience, several approaches appear promising and are described below.

First, if a patient has had an adequate trial of either an SRI or naltrexone as monotherapy (that is, as the only medication), the addition of the other medication appears to result in additional clinical improvement. A rationale for the use of serotoninergic and opioidergic agents in combination is to optimize the reduction in the addictive behaviors.

Martin, a sixty-one-year-old physician, came to our clinic because of an inability to stop gambling. "I've had this problem for a few years now. It's never really caused problems for me until the past year or two. My wife and my daughter have demanded I get help." Martin proceeded to discuss how gambling had affected his life. "Before I started gambling, I was completely committed to my work. I would work from early in the morning until late at night. Then I started playing blackjack at the casino. At first it was sort of a challenge, but I never thought much about it. I would go whenever I felt stress from work or just wanted to get away for a while. But after a few years, I gradually developed these cravings to go to the casino. My work suffered, and I just didn't care as much about it. I went through about $300,000 over the last two or three years. That's about everything I own. My house was paid for and now has two mortgages. We have no savings. I even pawned some of my wife's jewelry that I gave her thirty or forty years ago."

Martin was started on naltrexone. Initially he described his urges to gamble as severe. After reaching 150 mg/day, Martin described his response to the medication: "The medication has helped me a lot. For one thing, I just feel much calmer every time I think about gambling. I still get urges, but they're much less and they don't bother me as much." Martin then went two months without gambling. After that time, I received a call from Martin's wife. He had apparently returned to the casino on two different occasions and again lost several thousand dollars that he had recently saved. When he next returned to the clinic, he talked about his relapse. "I'm not sure why I went. I think I get lonely. My wife has her friends. When I'm not working, I don't have a lot to do or many interests. I think I gamble to feel something." Paroxetine, an SSRI, was then added to Martin's medication regimen. Over time, his dose was gradually increased to 40 mg/day. For Martin, the combination of medications not only decreased his urges and thoughts about gambling, but also improved his overall mood. Martin has now been abstinent from gambling for over a year. The extent to which a combination of an SRI and naltrexone may be effective and well tolerated in the treatment of impulse control disorders in general requires additional investigation.

Second, a person who has failed to respond to either an SRI or naltrexone may be effectively treated with a mood stabilizer, either as monotherapy or as augmentation (added to the SRI or naltrexone). In our clinical experience, some patients with impulse control disorders, although not screening positive for a manic episode, exhibit symptoms consistent with cyclothymia (mood swings between depression and low-level mania) or other subclinical cycling mood disorders. In these people, lithium, valproate, or another drug with putative mood-stabilizing properties may represent an appropriate treatment option.

"I can't believe I can't stop this behavior. My husband is suing for custody of our children, claiming that I am unable to care for them. I know I've left them alone for periods of time, and that was wrong. But I'm not 'unfit.' This is an illness. I just can't stop myself." Evelyn continued to describe her compulsive shopping behavior. "I've lost everything. I have no money, no job, and now no family. And yet I keep spending money. I didn't see any of this coming. I was just buying a few things—over and over again. The hole I was digging got bigger and bigger. Soon I was just unable to crawl out. Even now, knowing the problems I have, I continue to dig myself in deeper. I'll probably be facing legal problems soon. I don't know how I'll get by."

Other than her almost daily shopping, Evelyn reported no other impulsive symptoms or symptoms consistent with mania. She was tried on naltrexone, two SRIs, and a combination of the two classes of medication, all without significant benefit. While keeping Evelyn on a moderate dose of naltrexone (100 mg/day), on which she reported some decrease in her cravings to shop, we added lamotrigine (Lamictal), an anticonvulsant that is often used as a mood stabilizer. With a slow increase to 150 mg/day, Evelyn was able to report that she suddenly lacked all interest in shopping. "It's as if I don't really care to buy things anymore. Maybe it's because I've been through so much recently, but I really feel different. The thought of shopping is just not with me." For the next year, Evelyn displayed none of her previous behavior. Although she had occasional episodes of mild shopping, the almost constant shopping sprees were gone.

Very little is known about the role of mood stabilizers, such as lamotrigine, in treating impulse control disorders. Additional investigations into pharmacological interventions for individuals with impulse control disorders and bipolar spectrum symptoms would be particularly informative in optimizing treatment strategies for this group of patients.

Third, the possibility of adding atypical antipsychotics to SRIs in SRI-refractory impulse control disorders warrants consideration. A rationale for the use of drugs targeting both the dopamine and serotonin systems in obsessive-compulsive disorder might similarly apply to impulse control disorders. Clinical data support the use of typical and atypical antipsychotic drugs as efficacious and well-tolerated augmenting agents in the treatment of obsessive-compulsive disorder.

Austin came to our clinic after having served ninety days in jail for shoplifting. "I've got to stop doing this. I was told you treat people who steal. Quite frankly, I'm not sure anyone can help me." After careful evaluation, it was clear that Austin suffered from kleptomania. He reported no history or symptoms consistent with antisocial personality disorder or any other psychiatric disorder except depression. "I get so down every time I think about how this has ruined my life. Who wants to hire someone who's been in jail three times? I've been telling my lawyer I can't control myself, that I'm not just some thief. Why should he believe me? Once you're marked as a thief, no one listens. They think it's all excuses. The problem is that they never seemed to notice the crap I steal—I was taking lots of garden supply stuff. I had stacks of it at home, and I don't even have a garden. I don't know why I was taking that stuff. I tried to tell them I couldn't stop myself, but no one cared."

Austin was started on paroxetine, an SSRI. After several weeks and several increases in his medication, Austin told me that his mood was much better. "I feel a lot more like myself. Not so stressed or irritable. The thoughts about stealing have gone down some, but they're still there. Sometimes I can't sleep because I'm thinking about stealing and these weird items I might steal. It's really bothering me." Risperidone, an atypical antipsychotic medication, was then added to Austin's paroxetine. At 1 mg twice a day, Austin was able to report that the thoughts of stealing had significantly diminished. "I might get a passing thought at night, but the medication is really helping to keep those thoughts out of my head." Although several medication adjustments were necessary over the next few months, Austin has not been stealing and has been able to stay out of jail.

As in the treatment of obsessive-compulsive disorder, our clinical experience suggests that the addition of atypical antipsychotic medications to SRIs may benefit many people with impulse control disorders. Further clinical experience and study is necessary to explore the potential of antipsychotic drugs as augmentation for SRIs in the treatment of SRI-refractory impulse control disorder.

Fourth, as we will discuss in the next chapter, cognitive and behavior therapy may be quite useful in the treatment of impulse control disorders. Combined pharmacological and cognitive behavior therapy is considered the optimal treatment strategy for many psychiatric disorders. In our clinical experience, people who fail to respond to medication alone or respond only partially are more likely to find relief with a combination of drug and cognitive behavior therapies. Future studies should explore directly the contributions of pharmacological and behavioral therapy to clinical improvement in combination treatment strategies for impulse control disorders.

Relapses and Maintenance Treatments

Even with successful treatment of impulse control disorders, relapses should be expected. Relapses may occur for many reasons, but the ones we most commonly encounter are that the medications become less effective over time and that people fail to keep taking their medications. Why a person who improves on medications, feeling either reduced urges or no urges to engage in impulse behavior for several months or years, then experiences a resurgence of urges and impulsive behavior is not clear. This phenomenon has also been seen in the treatment of other psychiatric illnesses, such as depression or manic depression. Often, symptoms can be easily controlled by making simple adjustments in the dosage of the medication that had previously been effective. At other times, however, changes or additions to the medication will be necessary.

The other reason for relapse is that people often choose on their own to stop taking their medications; this is referred to in the medical literature as *noncompliance*. Achieving compliance with medication treatment in impulse control disorders is often difficult and may present challenges for the patient, family members, and the physician. For example, people who are suffering from compulsive sexual behavior may not comply with treatment because medication may reduce or eliminate the thrill associated with the behavior. Similarly, with pathological gambling, kleptomania, and compulsive shopping there is an exciting aspect to acquiring money or possessions that often results in people not wanting to dull or prevent that feeling with medication. Scenarios such as these are also seen in patients with drug abuse.

What can be done to prevent relapse? The easiest answer to this question is that people with impulse control problems need to continue taking medications, often for several years. Because only scant data on the natural history of individuals with impulse control disorders exist, the optimal duration of treatment and rates of relapse associated with discontinuation of pharmacological treatment are presently not known. Thus, there are as yet no guidelines for the recommended duration of treatment for impulse control disorders. In our experience, however, many people relapse upon discontinuation of treatment with medications. Therefore, we recommend continuing medication for at least two or three years after a person's symptoms have been adequately treated. At that time, if the person wishes to stop the medication, he or she should be taken off the medication gradually with the help of a psychiatrist, as abruptly stopping medication may produce unpleasant physical symptoms. The other reason for a person to stop medication gradually under the care of a psychiatrist is that the medication can be quickly restarted at the first sign of returning symptoms.

Family and loved ones may also play a significant role in helping to prevent relapse. The person with an impulse control disorder needs to feel that staying on his or her medication and staying away from the addictive behavior can be as satisfying as the impulsive behavior was. This is difficult because of the intense pleasure that these behaviors often produce. Borrowing from the treatment of drug problems, we often suggest that the family or loved one use non–addiction-related rewards to maintain medication compliance. These rewards may be incorporated into the treatment in a contingency management fashion to substitute for drug-related rewards. For example, medication compliance may be rewarded by an evening out for dinner or a movie. These reinforcements may be even more important during high-risk times for the behavior, when a person may feel less like complying with treatment recommendations.

Also, some preliminary research of ours has suggested that medication compliance is often aided by significant others. People who have a family member or friend encouraging them to take their medication, spending time with them, and demonstrating support in the struggle to overcome the illness are less likely to stop taking their medication and less likely to relapse into previous addictive behaviors.

Concluding Thoughts about Medications

Although our understanding of the most efficacious treatments for impulse control disorders is still incomplete, SRIs are often effective, especially at doses comparable to those used for obsessive-compulsive disorder. Naltrexone is also an effective treatment for impulse control disorders, particularly for those people who have strong urges to engage in the particular behavior. If a person has had an adequate trial of either an SRI or naltrexone, the addition of the other medication may result in additional clinical improvement. A person who has failed to respond to either an SRI or naltrexone, however, may be effectively treated with a mood stabilizer, either by itself or in addition to the SRI or naltrexone. There is also the possibility of adding atypical antipsychotics to SRIs or naltrexone. And finally, people who fail to respond to medication alone or who respond only partially are more likely to find relief with a combination of medication and cognitive behavior therapies.

There are obvious pros and cons to treatment with medication. Medication may be a quick and safe means of treating the behaviors, urges, and thoughts associated with impulse control disorders. No single medication, however, is guaranteed to be effective for everyone, and therefore multiple medications may have to be tried before benefits occur. Even after several medications or combinations of medications have been tried, there may still be little, if any, benefit for a small percentage of people who suffer from these disorders. Also, there are side effects associated with medications, but most of these are mild and tolerable, and can be managed very effectively.

Medication should be considered by anyone whose impulsive behavior interferes with his or her life or who feels distressed by his or her behavior. The medications we have discussed have shown great promise in relieving this distress in a majority of the people who seek treatment. The medication plays a significant role in allowing people to change their behaviors. As we discuss in the next chapter, however, medication is not the only answer to an impulse control disorder. For many people, psychotherapy may also be used effectively, either by itself or in combination with medication.

9

Psychological Treatments for Impulse Control Disorders

Psychological Aspects of Impulse Control Disorders

People who suffer from impulse control disorders report that increased feelings of stress, a decrease in self-esteem, and a pervasive sense of shame often accompany the impulsive behaviors. People with these disorders feel powerless to stop themselves, and they often describe all of these feelings as being the direct result of this lack of control over their own thoughts, urges, and behavior.

"I haven't liked myself for so long—ever since I started to gamble," Ellen told me. "I used to think I had a lot going for me, that I was somebody special. Once I became a gambling addict, I lost all of that. Now, I can't stand to look myself in the mirror in the morning. I stole from my husband. I forced us both into bankruptcy. I lied to myself, telling myself that I was doing it to help the family and give my kids more things, but the truth was I just couldn't stop.

I don't think I can ever forgive myself for the trouble I've caused my family. I'm sure they can never forgive me."

We have only recently started exploring the effect of impulse control disorders on levels of perceived stress. In the case of people with pathological gambling and kleptomania, the levels of perceived stress appear higher than in people with other psychiatric disorders. In fact, the stress appears to be directly related to the impulsive behavior and not to other psychiatric or medical illnesses from which the person may also be suffering. When the impulse control disorder is treated, the perceived stress appears to decline to normal levels. One man who suffered from kleptomania described the stress in his life: "I couldn't sleep at night because of the anxiety or stress. I felt such guilt about stealing from stores. Also, I kept worrying that it would be worse tomorrow, that I would never be able to stop myself. What if I just kept stealing more and more? Anything seemed possible. I had no trust in what I would or wouldn't do. Since being treated with naltrexone, I've actually slept the whole night through for the first time in years."

People with impulse control disorders report that they feel stress as a result of their inability to control their behavior. In part, the stress comes from not being able to predict whether they are going to engage in disruptive behavior. The stress is also due to the problems caused by the actual behavior. Pathological gambling and compulsive shopping usually result in severe financial and familial stress. Kleptomania may lead to the additional stress of legal consequences. Compulsive sexual behavior may cause relationship problems and even health difficulties secondary to sexually transmitted diseases. Clearly, further understanding of this important psychological complication of impulse control disorders is needed.

Low self-esteem is an almost universal consequence of impulse control disorders. Although no formal studies of this have been performed, we often hear reports of low self-esteem from people with impulse control disorders. One woman suffering from compulsive shopping told me, "How can I think much of myself when I can't even control what I do? It's like being a child—expecting to be gratified without regard for consequences. The problem is that I'm a middle-aged woman. The self-esteem problem has also affected my relationship with my husband and with my coworkers. I don't believe in myself any longer."

Low self-esteem may also set in motion a vicious cycle of behavioral addiction. It is not uncommon for people to report that when they have these feelings of low self-esteem or feelings of worthlessness, they develop thoughts of or urges to engage in impulsive behavior. One man described how his self-esteem was connected to his gambling behavior: "I tend to go to the casino when I hate myself. It usually starts with me thinking about how I've screwed up my life with the gambling. Then I feel really down. I'm sitting in my living room, depressed. Suddenly, I feel these cravings to gamble. Maybe I think it'll cheer me up, or maybe I just don't care anymore. Either way, I'm in the car and driving to the casino." Many people tell us that their urges to engage in the impulsive behavior are triggered when they are in a depressed mood. Also, low self-esteem may result in decreased work productivity and even loss of employment. When this occurs, many people, feeling depressed and having more unstructured time, will increase their impulsive behaviors.

Shame may contribute to both the low self-esteem and the stress that people with impulse control disorders feel. Most people with impulsive behavior blame themselves for their behavioral addiction. They may believe that they are "weak" for not being able to stop. Because many people view these behaviors as objectionable or even criminal, the inability to control their behavior may make some people feel immoral. For example, we commonly hear people with kleptomania refer to themselves as "evil" or "disgusting." One man with compulsive sexual behavior referred to himself as "vile": "I have these desires all the time. No normal person feels like this. And the horrible thing is that I give in to the desire most of the time. A better person would be able to ignore these desires. I'm not a good person."

The shame also contributes to the social avoidance exhibited by many people with impulse control disorders. The majority of people we see do not tell their friends or family about their behaviors.

Instead, they make up lies about where they have been and what they have been doing. One woman, after losing a substantial amount of money gambling, told her husband that she had been mugged on the street and that the criminal had taken all of her money. Her husband called the police, and a lengthy investigation ensued. The woman never told her husband or the police about the lie. "I didn't want someone else to get into trouble. That's why I was vague about details—you know, his size, hair color, and things like that. But I think if I had to get some stranger into trouble or tell my family the truth about the gambling, I'd pick the former. I'm not proud of that fact."

It is common that when people engage in behavior that they then try to cover up, they will report almost constant worries about being exposed. As a consequence, these people may avoid friends, family, and work. One man who suffered from compulsive sexual behavior described his concerns: "I tell my wife that I work late. That's when I'm out looking for sex. The trouble is that other times when I'm with my wife, I'm scared to see coworkers. I'm terrified that they'll say something that will show I've been lying. Because of this, I never go to social functions connected with work. Recently, I've been so nervous that I just tell my wife that we're not going out at all. I know she's upset—she thinks I'm ashamed of her. I can't tell her the real reason."

The social avoidance may in turn generate a cycle of repetitive impulsive behavior. Social avoidance may lead to isolation, loneliness, and depression, and people often respond by engaging in the behavior to a greater extent. Thus, therapy must consider the psychological impact of these disorders.

Cognitive Behavior Therapy

Traditional cognitive behavior therapies focus on the subjectively distressing symptoms of psychiatric illnesses. Impulse control disorders, however, involve behaviors that actually provide rewards or potential rewards to the person. As a result, researchers in cognitive behavior therapy have had to modify their therapeutic approaches or devise new, more creative approaches.

The scientific literature is rather limited when it comes to studies looking at the effectiveness of cognitive behavior therapy (CBT) in impulse control disorders. The evidence consists primarily of case reports (descriptions of a single patient) or case series (usually two or three patients). Probably the largest body of evidence deals with CBT's effectiveness for pathological gambling, whereas there is virtually no literature on whether CBT is effective for kleptomania. In our clinical experience, we find that CBT is often quite effective in treating these disorders. The emphasis of the therapy, however, differs somewhat depending on the impulse control disorder involved. We will discuss the basic principles of CBT, and then, drawing upon the literature of impulse control disorders, obsessive-compulsive disorder, and trichotillomania (urges to pull one's hair), we will describe how CBT may be useful for the various impulse control disorders.

CBT actually encompasses several approaches for changing the way a person thinks and behaves. The cognitive part of CBT addresses problematic or distorted thoughts. The behavioral element of CBT sees the behavior as a problem and focuses on the situational and emotional triggers as well as on the reinforcement mechanisms of the behavior. We will first describe the cognitive aspect of impulse control disorders.

Cognitive therapy addresses the mental events or thoughts that occur in response to an event in the environment and precede the person's behavioral response to that stimulus or event. These thoughts are often distortions of reality. They are also often automatic or habitual, and so the person is usually not aware of them. People with impulse control disorders may have irrational beliefs about the risks of the impulsive behavior, they have illusions of control over their behavior, and they have erroneous beliefs that the impulsive behavior is a solution to some problem in their lives. A person with kleptomania or compulsive shopping may believe that the act of stealing or shopping is actually within his control and that it is the only way for him to relieve anxiety. A pathological gambler may believe that she has control over whether she wins or loses because she selectively remembers only winning experiences. One sixty-year-old man who over the previous eight months had lost his entire savings through gambling told us, "I know that the odds favor the casino. I'm no fool. But I've won in the past with the system I've got [the system involved betting on roulette numbers corresponding to the ages of former girlfriends on specific days of the week]. I understand that the odds apply to most gamblers. But they don't apply to me."

The cognitive distortion may also involve specific situations that produce negative feelings. For example, when someone with compulsive sexual behavior believes that a certain work or family situation will be overwhelming, she may engage in sexual activities for relief. And finally, people may distort their thinking to give themselves permission for their behavior. A person who spends hours looking for sex may tell himself that he will look for sex "just a little" or "for just a few minutes" and then stop.

Cognitive treatment involves teaching people strategies for correcting their erroneous thinking. The person with pathological gambling may be instructed in probability and randomness. It may be necessary to discuss with the person with compulsive sexual behavior the idea that the event that felt overwhelming was in fact manageable and that the sexual activities not only do not relieve anxiety but may produce it. The person who steals may be reminded that she is distorting situations to give herself permission to initiate this behavior. One aspect of cognitive therapy involves monitoring of thoughts. People are instructed to keep daily thought records as a means of monitoring the thoughts associated with the impulsive behavior. The daily diary of thoughts actually heightens a person's awareness of faulty inner dialogues and helps him or her develop replacement thoughts that are more adaptive.

In addition to keeping a diary of thoughts associated with the impulsive behavior, people with impulse control disorders need to challenge their negative thoughts with actual data and alternative explanations. For example, Kristin reported that before she stole, she would often feel intense anxiety. When she had urges to steal, she rated her anxiety trigger as an 80 on a scale of 0 to 100. When asked to evaluate the thoughts associated with this anxiety, Kristin reported that she felt unable to control her relationship with her husband. Kristin was then asked to reevaluate her thoughts regarding her husband and her marriage. In fact, her marriage of seven years was actually quite stable. She and her husband had recently gone on vacation and had gotten along fine. Kristin thought about her relationship and was able to reduce her anxiety to 30. Now that she had reduced her anxiety concerning her husband, her urges to steal were also reduced.

Cognitive therapy generally consists of identifying and writing down the automatic thoughts and feelings associated with the impulse behavior and then challenging those thoughts with alternative thoughts. People are then instructed to practice these techniques every day, particularly when they are in states of emotional arousal (that is, when they are feeling anxious or depressed).

Although cognitive interventions alone may be effective in impulse control disorders, this has not been well studied. Generally, cognitive techniques have been incorporated with behavioral strategies in treating these disorders. There are several types of behavioral interventions.

Behavior therapy is based on the ideas of both operant and classical conditioning. That is, behaviors that are followed by a positive consequence or reward (such as money or a free item) tend to be repeated. This is the principle of reinforcement. On the other hand, when a behavior is followed by negative consequences (police apprehension or bankruptcy), the behavior occurs less frequently and may eventually stop. Also, certain environmental cues may over time come to be paired with particular behaviors. For example, a pathological gambler may feel a strong urge to gamble every time he or she sees the billboard advertisement for the local casino.

Many people with impulse control disorders report that the behavior is a means of reducing uncomfortable feelings. For example, a person with compulsive shopping may report that his or her shopping behavior is a way of eliminating intense anxiety feelings that result from his or her work or personal life. One woman who suffered from kleptomania reported that stealing was relaxing: "I steal something when I feel overwhelmed by my life. I can't seem to stop myself. It sounds horrible, but it calms me down." This is a form of negative reinforcement, and the repeated recurrence of the negative reinforcement increases the likelihood that the person will continue the impulsive behavior. In some people with impulse control disorders who report that the behavior is a relief from discomfort, the behavioral technique of exposure and response prevention can be usefully borrowed from the obsessive-compulsive literature. A person is gradually exposed to the situation that produces the anxiety, but he or she is prevented from engaging in the behavior that eliminates this anxiety (the compulsive shopping, for example). Although initially anxious, the person gradually comes to realize that the anxiety decreases in intensity and that some degree of anxiety is tolerable. As a person is continually exposed to something that produces anxiety, he or she pays less attention to that stimulus. This is the process known as habituation.

Another version of behavioral therapy is known as habit reversal. The person must first identify the environmental stimuli and situations that generate the urges to engage in the impulsive behavior. These stimuli are often taken from the daily diary we discussed when we were dealing with cognitive therapy. Once the environmental cues have been determined, a competing response is substituted for the impulsive behavior. The competing response should be incompatible with the impulsive behavior. For example, habit reversal therapy for kleptomania might suggest that when a woman has the urge to steal, she should clench her fists for several minutes. This act would interrupt the act of stealing by keeping her hands occupied and therefore making her unable to steal an object.

Relaxation techniques, such as deep breathing exercises, are important in habit reversal therapy. Relaxation techniques are useful for coping with the discomfort a person feels when he or she is trying to resist the urge to engage in an impulsive behavior. One such technique is muscle relaxation. This process involves tensing the toes for about fifteen seconds, then relaxing them for the same amount of time. The person then gradually works through the entire body by focusing on muscle groups from the toes to the forehead. The person then lies still and sustains the feelings of relaxation.

Stimulus control is another behavioral strategy that may reduce impulsive behavior. This technique relies upon modifying the environment to decrease the opportunities to engage in the impulsive behavior. Again, this strategy focuses on the environmental and situational cues that give rise to the behavior. For example, a person who feels the urge to steal when shopping alone at the grocery store may benefit from avoidance of the store. If someone else in the home is able to do the grocery shopping, then the person does not have to expose her- or himself to the stimulus. However, in situations where the cues cannot be completely avoided, stimulus control techniques such as shopping with someone else can be employed. Strategies must be shaped for the individual based on that person's cues and social situation. Success with this strategy will also depend upon on how easily it can be implemented with the least disruption to a person's life. Emily gambled only on weekend nights when she was bored and lonely. After she was started on medication, her urges to gamble were reduced, but she continued to gamble, although less often and for shorter periods of time. Emily decided to join a book club that met every Saturday night at the same time as she would normally have gone to the casino. Once she was able to distract herself with an enjoyable alternative, as well as continuing with medication, Emily quit gambling entirely.

Reinforcement of more appropriate behaviors may also decrease unwanted impulsive behaviors. In this therapy, rewards are used to increase the frequency of desired behavior or decrease the frequency of undesired behavior. Although impulsive behaviors provide gratification or pleasure when the person engages in these behaviors, low self-esteem, shame, and guilt are usually present as well. These "costs" of the behavior may increase over the course of the illness, and may actually come to exceed the pleasure associated with the behavior. A system can then be implemented that rewards the decreased frequency or absence of the behavior. Family members and friends may become part of the therapy by monitoring compliance and providing additional reinforcers, such as praise, for not engaging in the unhealthy behaviors. This technique should be incorporated with competing response or stimulus control therapy so that people can optimize their ability to manage the situations that trigger their urges.

The alternative to rewards is the loss of something positive whenever a person engages in the undesired behavior. This is called response cost therapy. To implement this strategy, desired activities or items need to be identified. A point system can then be linked to the behavior. By engaging in the behavior, a person loses desired items to a degree proportional to the frequency and intensity of the impulsive behavior.

Another behavioral treatment approach is aversion therapy. This therapy pairs an actual adverse consequence with the urge to engage in the impulsive behavior or with the behavior itself. This therapy is based on the idea that if the behavior results in more immediate negative consequences than positive outcomes, it is more easily extinguished. One example of a negative consequence might be snapping oneself on the wrist with a rubber band every time the urge to engage in an impulsive behavior is felt. In order for this to work, however, the person must be aware of the urges before actually engaging in the behavior and must be willing to use the rubber band.

Another form of therapy using negative consequences is covert sensitization. In this treatment, instead of actually experiencing a negative consequence, the person is asked to imagine it. For example, a person suffering from compulsive sexual behavior might imagine contracting AIDS or being arrested every time he or she has urges to engage in sexually promiscuous behavior. A variation of this, imaginal desensitization, has a person imagining various situations that give rise to the undesired behavior, but instead of imagining an aversive outcome, the person imagines that he or she can successfully avoid the behavior.

Although CBT may be quite effective in some people initially, a return of impulsive behavior should be expected, particularly in response to new stressful situations. Controlling this return of symptoms can usually be managed by reviewing the techniques that were successful in the past and practicing them again.

How well does CBT work for impulse control disorders, and if it does work well, what version of this therapy is most effective? There are no definite answers to these questions. In the case of pathological gambling, different versions of CBT, incorporating all of the behavioral strategies just discussed, have been tried, with varying success rates. Robert Ladouceur of Université Laval, Quebec, Canada, has reported success with cognitive therapy. Most of the CBT work in pathological gambling has been borrowed from research on obsessive-compulsive disorder. As more is known about pathological gambling, new versions of CBT are being developed. Nancy Petry of the University of Connecticut has been a leader in developing forms of CBT that are relevant to pathological gambling and reports good success with a form of CBT that provides increased reinforcement when the person does not gamble. Currently, there is no definitive version of CBT for these disorders. Depending upon where a person goes for treatment, there may be large differences in the type of CBT he or she receives.

The particular type of impulse control disorder may also determine the form of CBT that is most effective. In the case of kleptomania, there is no scientific literature addressing which treatment is most effective. However, it would be reasonable to believe that a form of CBT that incorporates a habit reversal strategy should be effective. CBT using exposure and response prevention therapy may be effective in the treatment of compulsive shopping. A combination of covert/imaginal sensitization and exposure and response prevention may be useful for kleptomania and for compulsive sexual behavior.

One of the inherent differences between impulse control disorders and other psychiatric disorders is that engaging in impulsive behaviors brings excitement, and for this reason, cognitive behavior therapy may be more challenging. Because of this excitement, many patients are simply unwilling to come forward for treatment or will postpone the treatment. Also, the rate of compliance with treatment is lower than the rate seen for psychiatric treatment in general. And finally, the risk of recidivism is higher than in other psychiatric disorders.

Although cognitive behavior therapy appears to be a promising treatment for impulse control disorders, our knowledge of its effectiveness is still preliminary, as there are few published data and virtually no controlled studies. However, in our clinical practices we find it useful for some people with impulse control disorders and consider it a promising approach, particularly when used in combination with medication.

Other Psychological Treatments with Possible Benefits

There is even less information concerning the effectiveness of other psychological treatments: psychodynamic psychotherapy, group therapy, self-help, and hypnosis. Given the extreme distress of people with impulse control disorders, we stress that some treatments appear to be more effective than others. In particular, treatment with medication should always be considered, either alone or in combination with cognitive behavior therapy. The following treatments appear to be useful for some people when combined with medication and/or cognitive behavior therapy. Generally speaking, they do not appear to be effective when used alone. However, these strategies have not been systematically studied, and so definitive judgments about their effectiveness cannot be made at this time.

Psychodynamic psychotherapy is a therapy that focuses on previous life events and relates them to the current symptoms. The development of insight through therapy is expected to aid in the change of behavior. This therapy suggests that impulsive behaviors are symptoms or expressions of underlying psychological conditions. Although the scientific literature contains case reports describing the benefit of this treatment for the individual impulse control disorders, there are no studies evaluating the effectiveness of this treatment. In our clinical experience, we have seen many people who have had years of insight-oriented psychotherapy, only to report no improvement in their impulsive behavior. Therefore, we cannot recommend this approach without the concomitant use of medications and/or behavioral therapy. However, although we do not recommend it as the sole treatment for impulse control disorders, insight-oriented psychotherapy may be effective in treating the shame, low self-esteem, and stress that are related to these disorders. Studies looking at this treatment, particularly in combination with medications, are necessary and overdue.

Group behavioral treatment, although it has received little attention, may have potential utility. Although empirical data are lacking, group therapy has been used in the case of compulsive sexual behavior, reportedly with good success. The true usefulness of group therapy for impulse control disorders, however, remains unsettled.

Self-help groups encompass organizations such as Gamblers Anonymous and Shoplifters Anonymous. These programs, modeled on the twelve-step program of Alcoholics Anonymous, are increasing in popularity, but whether they are effective is still unclear. The literature on Gamblers Anonymous (GA) is far from definitive. While some have reported that abstinence rates are increased with GA attendance, others report that dropout rates from GA are high and that abstinence rates in the long term (one to two years) are low. There is even less information on Shoplifters Anonymous or Sexaholics Anonymous.

Many people with impulse control disorders find these types of support groups helpful. Whether they are in fact helpful for the impulsive behavior itself may depend upon on the particular group. I recommend GA and Shoplifters Anonymous to my patients, but always in addition to the core treatments I've described (medication and cognitive behavior therapy).

Finally, a word should be said about less conventional treatments: hypnosis or trying harder to quit. Hypnosis has been described in case reports as improving trichotillomania, a similar type of impulsive behavior. Hypnotherapists induce an altered state of consciousness in a person in order to change his or her behavior. An altered state of consciousness is similar to deep relaxation. While relaxation techniques may be useful when combined with cognitive behavior therapy, there is no scientific evidence that they are effective when used alone.

Trying harder to stop the impulsive behavior, if done without medication and without therapy, does not appear to be effective. Most of the people we see have been trying hard for years to stop their behavior, without success. In fact, when used alone, this approach has the ability to make people worse. Many people feel like failures because of their inability to quit. In response, they may become more depressed and hopeless. Therefore, trying harder should include a commitment to seek psychiatric treatment.

In summary, there is still more research to be done on the effectiveness of therapy in treating impulse control disorders. Given our limited knowledge on this topic, however, several points should be made. Cognitive behavior therapy is a safe and potentially effective treatment that requires a commitment on the part of the patient. A person who would like to avoid medications should try this approach first. Other types of therapy may be useful for related difficulties, but there is no evidence that they reduce the symptoms of impulse control disorders if used alone. And finally, although there is some evidence that cognitive behavior therapy may be effective in treating impulse control disorders, at this time treatment with a combination of therapy and medications appears to yield the greatest chance of success.

10

Family, Friends, and Impulse Control Disorders

Growing Up with a Parent with an Impulse Control Disorder

Sheila, a twenty-two-year-old woman, wrote me a letter discussing her father's gambling problem and how it affected her family. "I first became aware of my father's problem with gambling when I was about fifteen years old. I guess it had been going on for about two or three years before that, but he did a good job of hiding it from the family. I remember I found out because my parents were fighting. They had had arguments in the past, but nothing like this. My father had lost a large amount of money. At first he didn't want to tell my mother how he had lost it, but it eventually came out: gambling. The problem was that the amount was beyond my family's ability to pay. Although my mother thought we had money in the bank, in our savings account, she discovered that it had also been drained by my father's gambling.

"The problem was that the fighting never seemed to end after that. My parents were always fighting—it seemed like something had been destroyed in their relationship. They were never the same couple again. The gambling didn't end, either. One time my father stole my mother's jewelry to get money for gambling. He even dug through my drawers one night to get extra cash. I remember my thoughts—how I despised him for ruining our family, and yet how I pitied and loved him in spite of the gambling. I didn't go to bed a single night that I wasn't awakened either by my parents fighting or by my mother crying.

"I watched this illness destroy my father and my family. He didn't go for treatment. Maybe he didn't know there was help or was just too scared to ask. My mother and I both took extra jobs to help repay the debts he had accumulated. The extra work prevented me from hanging out with my friends and doing much after school. I could never tell my friends. They had always liked my dad. I guess I didn't want his image ruined. I was also too ashamed to tell them.

"My mother told me that she could never trust him again. I think I felt the same way. My mother finally divorced him, and we went to live in another town. I never had a lot of contact with him after that. The gambling continued, and he never lived up to his promises to visit or call. About a year ago he killed himself.

"I have a lot of mixed feelings about this illness. Maybe nothing would have helped my father. I don't know. We sure didn't know what to do or how to get him to stop. It definitely robbed me of my adolescence. But the biggest problem was that it robbed me of a father and of my family."

Marriage and the Effects of an Impulse Control Disorder

We receive numerous phone calls from people all over the world asking for advice about friends or family members who may be suffering from an impulse control disorder. Many of the stories are quite moving. Family and friends are often unable to get the person into treatment, and so the calls may simply be seeking more information about these disorders and/or advice about how the family or friends can best cope with the emotional effects of the illness. Many people call only once. Others may call back to let us know the outcomes of various interventions. The following is the story of a man's long journey to find treatment for his wife.

"My wife was recently arrested for stealing from a local department store. I have known this woman for ten years, and I didn't think she was capable of such things. At first she was really ashamed to talk about the incident, but when she was able, I heard the most shocking story I could ever imagine. My wife had been stealing for the last fifteen years. This had been a secret she had carried with her all that time. Initially I felt shocked, angry, and betrayed. What else hadn't she told me? What little faith she had in me or in our relationship that she kept this a secret. Was there something wrong with me that prevented her from confiding in me? I said some unkind things at first. I was so hurt. And I was ready to leave.

"But I love my wife, and I had to figure this out. I was also incredibly sad that my wife had been living with this pain for so long and that I hadn't been able to see it or to help her. I didn't even know it was a disease. I kept thinking that she must be on drugs or something. She explained to me that she couldn't stop herself—that when she had urges to steal, she couldn't resist them. We spent a lot of time crying. I then decided that I was going to find help for my wife.

"We first went to our local primary physician. She had never heard about people who couldn't control their stealing. She thought my wife might be suffering from anxiety, and so she prescribed some antianxiety medication. At first, I thought the doctor was probably right. I hoped the medicine would help. About two weeks later, I came home to find my wife on the floor of our bedroom with a knife in her hand. She told me that she had been stealing again. She felt so ashamed that she wanted to kill herself. I didn't know what to do.

"We next went to a local psychiatrist. My wife found it difficult to talk about her stealing. She felt that the psychiatrist didn't believe her when she mentioned the urges she couldn't control. He told her to stop stealing things. She felt humiliated and judged. He gave her an antidepressant and told her she didn't have to come back for several months. The stealing continued.

"I started looking on the Internet for information about this problem. I still didn't even know what it was called. I read something about how therapy might work to stop people from stealing. We drove to the nearest large city and saw a therapist. The therapist told my wife to quit taking the medication, even though she was feeling less depressed on it. Instead, the therapist told her the stealing was a sign of intense anger and recommended weekly psychotherapy to understand where in her past the anger came from. Several months later, my wife was still stealing, and her feelings of hopelessness were more intense. This time I didn't get home in time, and my wife cut her wrists. She had to be hospitalized.

"Even in the hospital, no one seemed to know what to do about the stealing. In fact, it was largely ignored. The doctors treated her for depression, and she did get better. But the underlying problem was not being addressed. My wife and I mentioned it to the doctors, but they appeared disinterested or even somewhat judgmental. One of the doctors suggested that my wife might have some type of personality disorder or drug problem, even though I kept telling him that she had never had difficulties before and did not use drugs. She left the hospital in better shape, but the stealing continued.

"It was pretty easy to see how the stealing had taken a toll on my wife. She avoided stores almost completely. She stayed in the house, isolating herself from friends. She always seemed so hopeless. Her self-esteem was so low. Our marriage was also suffering. I wanted to help, but I didn't know how. I felt like a failure. She never wanted to be intimate, and this added to my own feelings of low self-esteem. We were drifting apart, and I didn't seem to be able to stop it. I started seeing my own psychiatrist for depression. Was there something I could say that would make her quit stealing and make her feel better? Was this all because of something I had said or done in the past? How could I let her live like this? I decided that someone must know something about this problem, whatever it was."

The man's search for a psychiatrist or psychologist who was familiar with kleptomania took him to four additional mental health professionals over a period of about two years. His wife felt that the previous physicians she had seen had never believed her when she told them about her urges to steal and her inability to resist those urges. When her husband contacted us, we gave him the name of a psychiatrist in his area and offered to speak with that person about how we treat kleptomania. We also recommended cognitive behavior therapy and family counseling. Although we did not treat his wife, he has contacted us several times over the past year and reported significant improvement in her stealing and in their relationship. "She's so much better. I can't tell you what your help has meant to us. I'm not sure you realize it, but you saved her life."

Misconceptions about Impulse Control Disorders

The concept of having an urge that cannot be restrained is alien to most people, and therefore many misconceptions about these disorders have been generated. In our experience, there is no basis for the misconceptions that we discuss here. If people with impulse control disorders are to seek treatment, it is important that their family, friends, and mental health professionals understand what is myth and what is fact concerning these disorders.

One popular belief is that the impulsive behavior is just a phase or that there is no problem because the person has not had serious consequences as a result of the behavior. For instance, parents might see stealing as a phase that adolescents go through. Gambling might be considered a harmless pastime because the person has not lost a lot of money. Excessive shopping might be excused because the person has been feeling down and needed a boost. While in many cases these statements may be true, they may also suggest a larger underlying problem. Many people with kleptomania start stealing in adolescence, and many pathological gamblers who have intense urges and severe preoccupations with gambling that interfere with their lives and result in low self-esteem may not appear to family or friends to have a problem. People with compulsive shopping often shop more when they are depressed or anxious. Family members may not be aware of the excessive shopping on other occasions. This is not to say that everyone who gambles, steals, or shops has a psychiatric illness. Family and friends, however, should be aware that people with impulse control disorders often excuse excessive or problematic behavior, and that it is not until the behavior becomes severe that a person seeks treatment.

Another prevalent view is that the impulsive behaviors are simply "bad" behaviors that a person can control but chooses not to. Family and friends may therefore chastise a person who suffers from one of these disorders, trying to shame the person into quitting. Parents may try harsher punishments at home to get their child to stop stealing or shopping. The idea that these behavioral addictions might be psychiatric illnesses is inconceivable to many people. Parents may see the behaviors as a sign of the child's defiance toward them. Spouses or friends may see the behaviors as anger directed toward them. When these behaviors are viewed in this way, most friends and family become angry and fail to support the person who is suffering from a severely disabling and shaming illness. Punishment, not treatment, becomes the way of dealing with the problem for many families. But these are psychiatric illnesses. People with impulse control disorders need and deserve the support and help of their family and friends. Punishment does not change these behaviors.

One final misconception concerning impulse control disorders is that the behavioral addiction is merely a symptom of an underlying emotional problem or a symptom of a traumatic childhood. This is often the view of mental health workers who are unfamiliar with impulse control disorders. They may suggest that someone who exhibits these behaviors needs to have addressed an underlying psychological problem rather than the behavior. Although many people with impulse control disorders may in fact have psychological problems or may have had difficult childhoods, most of the people we treat are high-functioning people with no significant underlying problem or childhood trauma that would explain the behavioral addiction. Family, friends, and the people suffering from these disorders should know that there is no research suggesting that impulse control disorders are a manifestation of an underlying psychological or childhood problem, and should realize that treatment that approaches the problem in this way may not be effective in reducing the behavior.

Advice for Family and Friends

Impulse control disorders may have a significant impact on the family and friends of someone who is suffering from such a disorder as well as on the person him- or herself. Family and friends often ask us what they can do to help such a person, what they should or should not say, and how they can learn to cope with this illness.

Many people will not disclose the fact that they have an impulse control disorder. Family and friends may not know how to be supportive or how to decrease their loved one's suffering. The strategies we discuss here are not treatments for these disorders. Medication and cognitive behavior therapy are the treatments to seek. Instead, these coping and advice strategies may enhance the effectiveness of treatments and may help to counteract the feelings of helplessness and hopelessness that may affect family and friends as well as the people who suffer from these disorders.

"I never knew what Robert was up to," Melissa began describing her husband's gambling. "He would be gone all night several times a week. He never told me where he'd been or what he had done. He became so secretive. I assumed he must be cheating on me. After several months he woke me in the middle of the night. He was crying. I had never seen him so fragile, so scared. He told me that we were deeply in debt and that we might have to file bankruptcy. At first I thought our investments must have turned sour. Imagine my horror and surprise when he admitted that he had lost everything gambling. I didn't know how to deal with that news. On one hand I was relieved that he wasn't having an affair. But on the other hand, I felt so deceived, hurt, and angry. Robert had a secret life that I had no knowledge of. Did he not trust me enough to tell me about the gambling? And how dare he ruin our family by stealing from me and the children? But I also felt sorry for him and wanted to comfort him in his pain. I have never been so torn in my response to someone. I loved and hated him simultaneously. Was I supposed to be the caring supportive wife or should I have walked out on him?"

Family and friends may have conflicting feelings about the person with an impulse control disorder. Unlike other illnesses that evoke sympathy, impulse control disorders may also anger loved ones because of the potentially destructive nature of the addictive behavior. A person who steals, gambles, has multiple sexual partners, or shops compulsively may affect family members financially, emotionally, or legally. Even when a person has controlled his or her behavior, the legal and financial consequences may continue for quite some time. For example, it is not uncommon for someone to embezzle from work to pay gambling debts. Several months after abstaining from gambling, however, a person may suddenly face criminal charges for those earlier actions. These are not illnesses that generally only affect one person — they disrupt families, and they may do so long after the illness is controlled.

There are no studies describing the effects of impulse control disorders on families or the needs of family members in dealing with such illnesses. In our practices, we routinely meet with family or loved ones when treating patients with impulse control disorders. This in turn has helped us identify and foster practices that enable families to navigate through the crises and prolonged difficulties associated with these disorders.

First, family and friends should educate themselves about these disorders. There is significant misinformation and ignorance about impulse control disorders in the medical community and among the general public. Educating themselves about these illnesses will allow family and friends to take the disorders seriously. All of these disorders are serious psychiatric illnesses that can significantly disrupt a person's life. Some people with impulse control disorders attempt to minimize their problem to their family and friends. Family and friends, in turn, may be unsure whether they should seek treatment for their loved one. Having information on these disorders allows family and friends not only to educate the person who is suffering but also to better understand what sources of treatment are available for the person. This knowledge offers both the person who suffers from the disorder and his or her family and friends hope that the behavior can be successfully controlled.

Second, family and friends should talk openly about the illness. Part of this communication should involve sharing knowledge about the disorder. Another aspect of this open communication is to force family and friends not to minimize the illness. Many family members may feel responsible for the person's behavior—for example, family members may wonder whether the way the parents raised the child or the way in which siblings interacted caused the disorder. By not addressing the illness, many family members may hope to avoid feeling guilty. I hope we have conveyed throughout this book that impulse control disorders are psychiatric illnesses, and that family members are not "to blame" for the disorders. Talking openly about these illnesses with knowledge about them should prevent family and friends from minimizing the seriousness of these disorders and thereby enable people with these disorders to seek treatment.

Dennis described his wife's kleptomania in these terms: "I knew she was stealing, but I just couldn't say anything about it. I guess I thought if I was a better provider she wouldn't steal. I felt it was my fault. If I mentioned it to her, I was worried that I would have to hear about how I had failed. I was too scared to face that sort of criticism. So I never said anything, even though I knew it was tearing her up inside."

Shirley never spoke to her son, Brian, about his gambling problem. "I thought I had failed him as a mother. By not talking about the gambling I could pretend he was O.K. and that I had done nothing wrong. The problem was that I didn't try to get him help until he had hit bottom. Should I have done something different when he was younger? I think of all the mistakes I probably made."

Third, family and friends should be supportive of the person with an impulse control disorder. This may be particularly difficult in cases where the person has betrayed the trust of family and friends. Many family members recoil instantly when we suggest being supportive. When I did this in the case of a compulsive shopper, her husband, Jason, told me, "How can I support her? She's lied to me. She's been selfish, and she's destroyed our family. I'm so angry and hurt, and you want me to support her? What about some support for me and her children?" This type of intense, hurtful, and angry response is quite normal, and family who feel this way should not feel guilty because of their response. These are difficult issues for both the patient and the family, and there's no absolutely right way for either the patient or the family to respond to these illnesses.

Supporting a person with one of these disorders, however, does not mean encouraging or even overlooking the behavior. It is simply important not to blame the person for the impulsive behavior, as blaming does not stop the behavior. Also, given that most people with these disorders suffer severe shame and guilt, the unconditional love of family can be beneficial and can significantly improve the chances that the person will voluntarily seek and commit to treatment.

The support of family and friends may also take the form of encouragement when the person makes a small step toward improvement. Congratulating someone when he or she has gone a first week without stealing or celebrating a pathological gambler's perseverance in attending therapy for the first month are ways in which family can support patients in a healthy manner. Successful treatment of these disorders may take months or years and often requires trials of multiple medications and weeks or months of therapy. This can lead to discouragement on the part of the person suffering from the disorder and on his or her family. Family and friends need to maintain hope. In fact, the majority of people with these disorders improve with treatment. Time and patience, however, are often required. Thus, family and friends need to be helpful in encouraging compliance with treatment.

Family and friends are often impatient with the pace of a person's improvement. They may feel a need to offer solutions and feel frustrated by the slowness of the improvement. This is another reason why family and friends should educate themselves about effective treatments and about treatments that have been shown not to work or that can even worsen the disorder.

The support of family and friends should not, however, take the form of encouraging the behavior or helping the person avoid the consequences of the behavior. For example, many pathological gamblers and people with compulsive shopping often ask family members for money. "He told me that he needed the money to pay debts or he would have trouble with certain people," Debra began to describe her brother's gambling problem. "I had to give him the money. What if something happened to him? I would feel guilty that I could have prevented it with a little financial help. Of course, after I gave him the money, he went right to the dog track and lost every penny. Now I feel so stupid. But if it were to happen again, I'm not sure I wouldn't do it all the same way. Should I turn my back on family?" This is a difficult situation to address. In most cases, family and friends should not enable the person to continue the behavior. Family and friends may feel guilty, particularly when the person pleads for one final gamble or tells the family that he needs to win in order to avoid all sorts of horrible consequences. Instead of money, family and friends should provide support for the person by offering to help her seek treatment and by encouraging her during treatment. People with kleptomania may ask family members to assist them by hiding stolen property or lying to the police. They may also tell their family members that they will now stop their behavior and that they have finally learned their lesson. Although this may sound appealing, people with kleptomania do not just stop their behavior. Hiding stolen property or lying to the police not only is against the law but also will not help the person who is suffering from kleptomania. Family members should not become implicated in the adverse consequences of a loved one's behavior. Supporting a person with an impulse control disorder does not mean ruining one's own life to help a loved one avoid the consequences of his or her actions.

Family and friends often ask what they should or should not say to someone with an impulse control disorder. This is difficult to answer, as it will differ from individual to individual. In general, however, words of blame ("What's wrong with you?"), comments that minimize the problem ("You'll get over it"), suggestions that the person lacks willpower ("Why can't you quit? I heard about someone else who quit"), or phrases that evoke guilt ("Do you know how this affects your family?") or shame ("I can't believe you can't stop this") are rarely helpful. Instead, words of support and love are important and helpful in improving the person's self-esteem. Family and friends should let the person know that they are supportive and willing to talk about the problem.

In some cases, people with impulse control disorders refuse treatment and refuse to admit that they are suffering from an illness. Zachery brought his son, Daniel, to our clinic for his gambling problem. After an interview it was clear that Daniel suffered from pathological gambling. He was also experiencing severe financial problems and was in jeopardy of losing his job because of the gambling. His marriage had also suffered. However, Daniel was adamant in his refusal of either medication or therapy. He wanted no interventions. "I will just stop on my own," he told me. "I don't need any help." In cases such as these, family and friends may have little recourse but to allow the person to continue his or her self-destructive behavior. Many people with impulse control disorders do not seek treatment until they have hit rock bottom. For some, this may mean losing their savings, their home, their marriage, and their children. This is often difficult for family and friends to watch. It is important that family and friends continue to assert the need for psychiatric treatment and to affirm their support for the person and their understanding of the disorder. When this becomes too difficult emotionally for family and friends, they may need to seek treatment or counseling for feelings of guilt and/or helplessness.

Family and friends should consider therapy for themselves as a way of coping with the burden of an impulse control disorder. The recognition or discovery of an impulse control disorder in the family often leads to a period of great vulnerability and uncertainty. Family members often feel that the illness has taken a certain amount of control away from them. For example, the father with pathological gambling who lies and loses large amounts of money disrupts the family's sense of financial and emotional security. Furthermore, the inability to protect a family member or friend from a disabling illness such as kleptomania may disrupt the family members' identities as protectors. The family may feel failure and violation. Even when the illness is treated, family members may retain an intense feeling of life's uncertainty that in turn may prevent them from living normal lives. As the family then searches for ways to reestablish control in their lives, certain adaptive skills may be necessary.

Family members need to learn about the illness in order to achieve mastery over the disorder's effects on the family. "I had never heard of compulsive shopping," Evan explained as he described problems with his wife. "As the debts piled up, I didn't know what was happening. I told my wife that her shopping was out of control, but she continued anyway. I didn't know if she was crazy, hated me, or was too stupid to know what she was doing. After reading about compulsive shopping, I finally realized what my wife was going through, and we sought appropriate treatment." Family members also need to learn to deal with the symptoms of the disorder and to have a working relationship with the health professional in charge of the family member's care. Because impulse control disorders often result in feelings of betrayal within the family, the creation of alliances to deal with the illness is necessary. For example, feeling like one has allies among health professionals in the battle against these illnesses may help overcome feelings of helplessness and vulnerability. A working alliance with the health-care provider may also decrease the feeling that the future is uncertain and increase the hope for recovery.

In the case of children or adolescents with an impulse control disorder, these same strategies apply—education, open communication, and support. In addition, however, parents need to be firm with their children concerning the need to stop these behaviors. Often, parents tend to overlook or minimize the illness, suggesting that the behavior is simply a "phase" young people go through. Parents face a difficult situation given that they cannot completely cut their children off financially or kick them out of the house due to the behavior. Given these limitations, parents must still teach their children that they are responsible for their behavior and that they will have to accept the consequences, regardless of the cause of the illness. Because children and adolescents may lie to their parents about these behaviors, it is also important that they understand that an illness is not an excuse for deception and that they must work to change the way they behave. Impulse control disorders appear to worsen over time if left untreated. Therefore, parents should be learn the symptoms of these disorders so that they can detect the problematic behaviors early in their children's lives and intervene with appropriate treatment as soon as possible.

In summary, impulse control disorders may have a significant impact on a person's relationships with family members and friends. It is therefore important that the person's family and friends educate themselves about impulse control disorders. There is help for those who suffer from these disorders. Family and friends can be a vital source of support and education for such people.

Advice for People with Impulsive Behavior

People with impulse control disorders suffer not only from the illness but also from the social isolation, shame, and sense of guilt associated with their behaviors. These disorders are illnesses not unlike diabetes or heart disease. The difference, however, is that these illnesses may affect a person's family and friends in a way that diabetes or heart disease do not—that is, they may cause loved ones to distrust, and even dislike, the person. Changing behavior may take time, and people suffering from impulse control disorders should understand this.

People who engage in impulsive behaviors must start by accepting the fact that they have an illness. This may be quite difficult. The behaviors may be associated with significant guilt for the way in which these people have behaved toward others. Keeping the behaviors a secret often allows these people to deny to themselves that there is a problem. If people who suffer from impulse control disorders want to change their behaviors, however, that change must start with an acknowledgment of the problem.

Kevin described his compulsive sexual behavior in these terms: "I kept telling myself that there was nothing wrong with me. This was in spite of the fact that I was constantly thinking about or looking for sexual partners even as my business crumbled. Instead, I actually told myself that the sexual behavior was good for me—it helped me relax—and that without it I couldn't be successful. I'm sure on some level I knew it was a huge problem, but admitting that was just too difficult. I think I felt dirty. It was only after my wife left me and I lost my retail company that I suddenly was able to admit to myself that I had a problem. I wish I had been able to admit it several years earlier."

As in the case of family and friends, people with impulse control disorders must educate themselves about the illnesses. People should talk with their physicians or therapists about their illnesses and read as much as they can. Education about the various impulse control disorders may help sufferers understand why they behave the way they do. This will allow them not only to appreciate past behaviors but also to guard against future impulsive behaviors. Additionally, a greater knowledge about the disorders allows people to make more informed decisions about the types of treatments available to them.

"I spent years stealing and never knowing it was an illness," Julia told me. "I can't begin to tell you how horrible I felt. I knew something was wrong in my head, and yet, all of the messages in society simply told me I was a thief. My minister kept asking me why I was so angry—he assumed that only angry people stole. I would go home and cry—I didn't feel like a thief and I didn't feel angry. Just finding out my behavior was an illness and that there were treatments that might work saved my life."

People with impulse control disorders must recognize that there are treatments available to them that show promise in alleviating their symptoms and improving their lives. Most people with impulse control disorders have difficulty trying to overcome their behaviors on their own. It is important to find health professionals knowledgeable about these illnesses so that people can receive the treatment best suited to their problem.

Having an impulse control disorder does not excuse the behavior associated with it. Although it may explain why a person acts a certain way, impulse control disorders do not let someone off the hook for illegal conduct, nor do they eliminate the pain that these behaviors often causes family and friends. Many people with impulse control disorders feel unable to control their urges to engage in certain behaviors. People with impulse control disorders did not bring the illness on themselves. They can, however, control their decision to seek help for the disorder.

Related to the recognition of the impulsive behaviors is the awareness that these disorders often affect loved ones. People with impulse control disorders lie to loved ones, they often steal from close friends, deceive family and friends, and they hurt the people who are trying very hard to understand and help with the illness. Recognizing the effects of the disorder on loved ones is usually quite painful. Working to mend these relationships may be crucial in dealing with the illness. Evidence suggests that people with strong support in their lives stay in treatment longer and therefore may respond better to treatment.

After being treated for gambling addiction, Gerard suddenly realized that he had lost all of his friends. "I lied to so many people.

I cheated anyone I could for a few extra dollars to gamble. My addiction—and I—ended up hurting a lot of people. Why should I have expected that anyone would be around when I got better? Sure it's an illness, but people have their limits. I don't blame them. The problem is that the loneliness often makes me think I might as well go back to gambling. What has getting healthy gotten me? Instead of thinking that way, however, I realize that I have to make a new life for myself. Part of that new life is trying to repair the relationships I've destroyed over the years."

Current information suggests that these disorders are lifelong illnesses if left untreated. Additionally, early evidence suggests that medication treatment for these disorders may be necessary for several years. Impulse control disorders are not the same as having a cold—they do not get better in a few days. Managing one's urges to engage in impulsive behavior may be an ongoing issue for many people. Acceptance of the chronic nature of these disorders is a necessary component of treatment.

Treatment generally cannot be effective unless a person follows the recommendation of his or her health professional. Margery was treated for pathological gambling with naltrexone, an opioid antagonist. After several weeks on the medication, she reported no urges to gamble and had successfully stopped gambling. After four months of abstinence, Margery decided to stop her medication. Within two weeks her urges came back, and she was gambling almost daily. Margery again started naltrexone, and her gambling ceased. Margery repeated this pattern of stopping and starting medication for several years, with similar results each time. "I just don't want to take medication," Margery told me. "I keep believing I can stop without medication. Although I have never been able to stop on my own, I keep thinking I can. It doesn't make sense."

This means that medication must be taken as prescribed and that the work associated with doing various therapies, such as cognitive behavioral therapy, must be performed as directed by the therapist. Many people with impulse control disorders want to be able to engage in the behavior "every now and then." Complete abstinence, however, should be the goal of treatment. This potential conflict between the health professional's goal (complete abstinence) and the person's private wishes (to do the behavior every so often) may result in a person not following the recommendations of the health professional. Acceptance of the goal of abstinence may be necessary for effective treatment to begin.

Finally, people with impulse control disorders need patience when seeking treatment. Although effective treatments are available, they are not effective for every person. "I quit going to my doctor after the first two medications failed to help me," Jerome told me. "I'm not waiting months to get my gambling under control. If they can't fix it in a few weeks, there's probably no hope for me." Although incorrect in his assessment of the treatment potential, Jerome's feelings are shared by many people with impulse control disorders. Both medications and therapy can take several weeks or months to yield results. Furthermore, health professionals may have to try several different approaches to treatment. This process of trial and error can be very frustrating for the patient. A person who desperately wants to get better may lose hope in the physician or therapist who appears to be making little improvement in his or her life. The person suffering from an impulse control disorder, however, may have to realize that improvement takes time. Our current knowledge about impulse control disorders is still limited. Patience and perseverance are needed when seeking treatment for these disorders.

In summary, people with impulse control disorders can find hope in the fact that there are treatments available to them that are often quite effective. An understanding of the particular disorder, its impact on others, the available treatment options, as well as the limitations of treatments, are all necessary elements if they are to pursue treatment and change their lives for the better.

Appendix A

Where to Get Help

Organizations Associated with Impulse Control Disorders

Association for the Advancement of Behavior Therapy
305 Seventh Avenue, Suite 1601
New York, NY 10001-6008
Telephone: 212-647-1890
Web site: www.aabt.org
(Behavior therapy referral source)

Compulsive, Impulsive and Anxiety Disorders Program
The Mount Sinai Medical Center
One Gustave L. Levy Plaza
New York, NY 10029
Director: Eric Hollander, M.D.
Telephone: 212-241-3623
Web site: www.mssm.edu/psychiatry/ciadp.shtml

Gam-Anon
P.O. Box 157
Whitestone, NY 11357
Telephone: 718-352-1671
Web site: www.gam-anon.org
(Referral source for family and friends of gamblers)

Gamblers Anonymous
P.O. Box 17173
Los Angeles, CA 90017
Telephone: 213-386-8789
Web site: www.gamblersanonymous.org
(National organization)

Impulse Control Disorders Clinic
University of Minnesota
Department of Psychiatry
2450 Riverside Avenue
Minneapolis, MN 55454
Telephone: 612-627-4879
Web site: www.med.umn.edu/psychiatry/research/impulse.htm

National Council on Sexual Addiction and Compulsivity
Web site: www.sca-recovery.org/

Obsessive Compulsive Foundation, Inc.
337 Notch Hill Road
North Branford, CT 06471
Telephone: 203-315-2190
Web site: www.ocfoundation.org

Obsessive-Compulsive and Related Disorders Clinic
Stanford University
Stanford, CA 94305
Director: Lorrin M. Koran
Telephone: 650-725-5180
Web site: http://ocdresearch.stanford.edu/index.html

Problem Gambling Clinic
Yale University
New Haven, CT 06520
Director: Marc Potenza
Email: marc.potenza@yale.edu

Program on Human Sexuality
University of Minnesota
1300 South Second Street, Suite 180
Minneapolis, MN 55454
Director: Eli Coleman, Ph.D.

Sexaholics Anonymous
Web site: http://www.sa.org

Shoplifters Alternative
380 North Broadway, Suite 306
Jericho, NY 11753-2109
Telephone: 800-848-9595
Web site: www.shoplifters.org

Shoplifters Anonymous
P.O. Box 24515
Minneapolis, MN 55424

Shoplifters Anonymous
507 Lawrence
Ann Arbor, MI 48104
Telephone: 313-913-6990

Shoplifters Anonymous
P.O. Box 5463
Concord, CA 94524-5463

Appendix B

Selected Books and Articles Related to
Impulse Control Disorders

General Interest

Lorrin M. Koran, *Obsessive-Compulsive and Related Disorders in Adults* (Cambridge: Cambridge University Press, 1999).

Compulsive Shopping

Don W. Black, "Compulsive Buying: A Review," *Journal of Clinical Psychiatry* 57 (suppl 8): 50–54 (1996).

Gary Christenson et al., "Compulsive Buying: Descriptive Characteristics and Psychiatric Comorbidity," *Journal of Clinical Psychiatry* 55: 5–11 (1994).

C. Wesson, *Women Who Shop Too Much: Overcoming the Urge to Splurge* (New York: St. Martin's Press, 1990).

Compulsive Sexual Behavior

Eli Coleman, "Is Your Patient Suffering from Compulsive Sexual Behavior?" *Psychiatric Annals* 22: 320–325 (1992).

Kleptomania

Marcus Goldman, *Kleptomania: The Compulsion to Steal—What Can Be Done?* (Far Hills, NJ: New Horizon Press, 1998).

Jon Grant and S. W. Kim, "Clinical Characteristics and Associated Psychopathology of 22 Patients with Kleptomania," *Comprehensive Psychiatry* 43: 378–384 (2002).

Susan McElroy et al., "Kleptomania: A Report of 20 Cases," *American Journal of Psychiatry* 148: 652–657 (1991).

Pathological Gambling

L. Berman and M. Siegel, *Behind the 8-Ball: A Guide for Families of Gamblers* (New York: Fireside Press, 1992).

Jon Grant and S. W. Kim, "Demographic and Clinical Features of 131 Adult Pathological Gamblers," *Journal of Clinical Psychiatry* 62: 957–962 (2001).

S. W. Kim and Jon Grant, "The Psychopharmacology of Pathological Gambling," *Seminars in Clinical Neuropsychiatry* 6: 184–194 (2001).

National Research Council, *Pathological Gambling: A Critical Review* (Washington, D.C.: National Academy Press, 1999).

Appendix C

Frequently Asked Questions

Patients and their loved ones often have questions about impulse control disorders. These are the most frequently asked questions and the answers we provide our patients and their families. These questions are addressed in more detail throughout the course of the book. What follows are quick summaries of these issues.

How Can I Persuade My Spouse to Go to Treatment?

People with impulse control disorders often create severe distress for loved ones and yet do not believe they need treatment. We recommend that families start by telling their loved one how his or her behavior has affected the family. This should be done in a matter-of-fact fashion without blaming the person but also without minimizing the effects. Family members may want to educate the person about the illness in question and have treatment options available for the person in the form of phone numbers or addresses. Many people refuse treatment regardless of the actions of family. These people may need to "hit bottom" before seeking treatment. If the person is resistant to treatment options, family members may need to focus more on what they themselves need (therapy, support groups, etc.) given the toll an impulse control disorder takes on them.

Will I Pass This Illness on to My Children?

There's some evidence that there may be a genetic component to at least pathological gambling. In fact, in many families, pathological gambling also appears related to alcohol problems. We simply know too little about the other impulse control disorders to make definitive comments. Nevertheless, in our clinical practices, it is quite common to have several family members with the same or similar disorders. The relationship of genes to environment, however, is quite complicated, and more research is needed on this topic.

Will This Problem Just Go Away on Its Own?

There's no evidence that impulse control disorders just spontaneously disappear. In fact, if left untreated, they actually appear to be chronic illnesses. This does not mean that people cannot stop the behavior for periods of time, sometimes relatively long periods, but the vast majority of people appear to start the same or similar behavior at some time in the future. One woman with kleptomania told me that she had waited forty years for her illness to go away. After eight months of various medication trials and cognitive behavior therapy, she got her wish.

Should I Tell Friends, Coworkers, or Family about My Problem?

Whether to tell others about impulsive behavior and how much to tell are very personal issues. Many people feel that they are being dishonest (lying by omission) with others by not mentioning their behavior. I advise people to question their motivation for telling others. If a person is looking for forgiveness or unquestioning support, he or she may have to be prepared for not getting the desired response. Family and friends may have difficulties with the information, and, therefore, educating them about the behavior will be necessary.

Will I Just Start Some New Addiction If This One Is Treated?

There appears to be some evidence that certain people simply shift addictive behaviors. Someone may have a problem with alcohol for years, and when treated suddenly start gambling. With proper education, treatment, and family counseling, the majority of our patients are able to control addictive behaviors of all sorts.

Will I Always Have This Illness?

No one knows enough to answer this definitely. We treat our patients as if these are chronic disorders, which the available evidence suggests is the case. People with impulse control disorders should try to accept these disorders as chronic. The illness can be managed but not cured. Even after a few years, when people may stop their medication and have no recurrence of their impulsive urges, they should still be mindful of previous stressors that gave rise to their urges and attempt to avoid them. The brains of people with impulse control disorders may always be more vulnerable to developing other impulse control disorders or redeveloping the same disorder.

What Kind of Person Do These Things Affect?

Stealing, gambling, shopping, and sex are behaviors that many believe people should be able to control. Those who cannot do so often feel that they lack willpower or moral character. Although the acts associated with these disorders are often personally painful as well as hurtful to others, these are psychiatric illnesses of the brain. We hope this book will disabuse people of the notion that a failing of character has anything to do with these disorders.

How Did I Get This Illness?

Although we are not sure of the cause or causes of these disorders, we hope that this book has shed some light on how complicated these illnesses are. Biology, genes, and environment may all be implicated in the etiology of these disorders. There does not appear to be any one single cause of impulse control disorders. Although we don't know why some people develop an impulse control disorder and others don't, we stress that for those with these illnesses there are some promising treatments.

Will I Ever Feel Normal?

Every patient who comes to see us for treatment either asks this question or hints at it with other comments. Impulse control disorders rob people of control over their own lives. Quality of life appears to be greatly diminished by these illnesses. Although we are still unable to make guarantees, we believe that given our current knowledge of these disorders we can offer hope.

Index

About the Authors

Jon E. Grant, J.D., M.D., is currently the Minnesota Medical Foundation's Endowed Research Fellow in the Department of Psychiatry at the University of Minnesota. Dr. Grant holds degrees from Brown University, Harvard University, Cornell University, University of Chicago, and the University of Michigan. He has written extensively on impulse control disorders.

S. W. Kim, M.D., is an associate professor of psychiatry at the University of Minnesota and a graduate of Catholic University Medical School in Seoul, Korea. For the past twenty years, Dr. Kim's research has focused on obsessive-compulsive disorder. Dr. Kim is a Life Fellow of the American Psychiatric Association.

Drs. Grant and Kim manage the Impulse Control Disorders Clinic at the University of Minnesota. They have pioneered research in the field of behavioral addictions. Their research has been supported by the National Center for Responsible Gaming and the National Institutes of Mental Health.